PSYCHOLOGY

IN BITE-SIZED CHUNKS

To Anne and Phillip
– psychological inspirations.

PSYCHOLOGY

IN BITE-SIZED CHUNKS

JOEL LEVY

Michael O'Mara Books Limited

First published under the title *Freudian Slips* in 2013
This edition first published in Great Britain in 2020 by
Michael O'Mara Books Limited
9 Lion Yard
Tremadoc Road
London SW4 7NQ

A CIP catalogue record for this book is available from the British
Library.

Papers used by Michael O'Mara Books Limited are natural,
recyclable products made from wood grown in sustainable forests.
The manufacturing processes conform to the environmental
regulations of the country of origin.

ISBN: 978-1-78929-235-0 in paperback print format

2 3 4 5 6 7 8 9 10

Illustrations by Greg Stevenson
Designed and typeset by K.Design, Winscombe, Somerset
Printed and bound by CPI Group (UK) Ltd, Croydon, CR0 4YY
www.mombooks.com

CONTENTS

INTRODUCTION

I F A MAN IN A GORILLA SUIT walked across your field of vision, would you notice him? Incredible though it may sound, there is roughly a fifty per cent chance that you would not notice the gorilla if you happened to be concentrating on something else. Known as the 'invisible gorilla' phenomenon, or inattentional blindness, this is just one of over fifty amazing and intriguing nuggets mined from the treasure trove of psychology and explained in this book.

Did you know, for instance, that Freud was addicted to cocaine, confessed to never having understood women, never said 'Sometimes a cigar is just a cigar', and believed that when you dream you are flying, your airborne body is a phallic symbol: a giant, flying erection? Did you know that newborn babies may be able to 'see' with their tongues; that

German stomach ulcers are nearly ten times more responsive to the placebo effect than Brazilian ones; or that, while psychologically healthy people cannot tickle themselves, schizophrenics with delusions of being controlled *can* tickle themselves?

Psychology in Bite-sized Chunks explains all these bizarre insights and fascinating trivia, exploring the most interesting and important concepts in psychology. It covers every aspect of this science, from psychoanalysis to behaviourism, counselling to neuroanatomy, personality to the paranormal. Difficult concepts are broken down and explained, illustrated with illuminating examples and analysed for their wider significance.

The book also explores the most important contributions of the most important contributors in the history of psychology, from Freud and Jung to Maslow and Reich, Laing and Pavlov to Adler and Zimbardo. Yet the discussion is always alert to intriguing trivia. Did you know, for instance, that the teenage nickname of Rorschach of ink-blot fame, years before development of his eponymous test, was Klex, German for 'ink blot'. Or that in the course of his research into conditioning in dogs, Pavlov succeeded in making a dog neurotic? You will learn about the Hawthorne effect, which is where people alter their behaviour when someone is watching, such as when male subjects tolerate higher levels of pain when being watched by an experimenter; and about the Baskerville effect, where superstitious beliefs can cause death. You will learn the truth about Project Pigeon, the outrageous but successful scheme to put pigeons inside missiles to guide them to their targets, and discover the farcical horrors of aversion therapy for homosexuality, including the true story of when psychiatrists in the 1960s claimed to have used 4,000 electrical shocks to turn a homosexual into a bisexual.

Technical terms are defined and explained as they arise, but an important distinction that is often poorly understood is worth acknowledging: the difference between the multiple terms derived from the root 'psych-'. What *is* the difference between psychiatry, psychotherapy, psychoanalysis and psychology? Psychology is the study of the psyche, the Greek word for 'mind'; this term encompasses all the different strands of philosophical and scientific enquiry into matters concerning the mind. Psychotherapy is the treatment of psychological problems and illness through methods involving psychology, and includes psychoanalysis and aspects of psychiatry. Psychiatry is the branch of medicine devoted to mental illness; it is practised by medical doctors. Psychoanalysis is both a theory of mental structure and function, and a method of psychotherapy. Traditionally, most psychoanalysts were expected to have been trained as psychiatrists, and the terms were often conflated.

ADLER AND THE INFERIORITY COMPLEX

ALFRED ADLER (1870–1937) WAS a doctor with an interest in psychology and education, who was invited by Freud to join the Vienna circle of psychoanalysts and for a time was designated as the heir apparent for psychoanalysis. However, Adler's theories rapidly evolved away from Freud's insistence on sex as the psyche's dominant drive, and the concomitant model of human psychology as primarily a product of past experiences, mainly those of early infancy. Adler believed that power was the true engine of the human psyche, particularly the power relations between people. For instance, he argued that sibling birth order is an important factor governing personality, a theory rapidly appropriated by folk psychology. The same fate befell many of Adler's concepts, none more so than the inferiority complex.

Everyone inevitably experiences some feelings of inferiority; Adler's insight was that such feelings could be the primary driver behind much of human psychology and behaviour, especially in the formative childhood years, as the psyche attempts to compensate for, adapt to, or overcome the feelings. A child who feels physically inferior, for instance, might pursue sports to overcome his feelings, or might turn away from physical activities altogether and become bookish. Adler cited the classical tale of Demosthenes, the great Athenian orator who overcame a childhood speech impediment by training himself to speak with stones in his mouth.

If the emotions and thoughts arising from normal inferiority feelings are suppressed and driven into the unconscious mind, the result may be an inferiority complex. A complex, in psychoanalytic terms, is a system of unconscious desires, thoughts and feelings that acts on the conscious mind, often in an unhealthy or unhelpful fashion. Adler was careful to draw a distinction between normal inferiority feelings and the maladaptive inferiority complex, but this distinction has been lost in the popular appropriation.

Freud took a dim view of Adler's focus on the psychology of power and inferiority, dismissing his developmental model as an 'infantile scuffle', amounting to little more than vulgar clichés such as 'wanting to be on top' and 'covering one's rear'. The relationship between the two men played out Adler's own theory, with Adler lamenting that he was always 'forced to work in [Freud's] shadow'. Their split turned into a vicious feud, and in 1911 Adler set up his own school of psychoanalysis, which came to be known as Individual Psychology. For a time he became a world-famous intellectual figure and bestselling author, but his time as the 'rock star' of psychoanalysis passed and he died a lonely death in Aberdeen while on a lecture tour. Although his name is little known today, his legacy is widespread in modern psychotherapy and his theories and terms have infiltrated many aspects of popular psychology.

ARCHETYPES AND THE COLLECTIVE UNCONSCIOUS

In Jungian psychoanalysis, archetypes are embodiments of beliefs/concepts/experiences, which are common to all human psyches and may even be aspects of the underlying nature of reality. Although each individual experiences/encounters an archetype in different forms, the basic seed/scaffold of the archetype is located in the unconscious. Jung believed that since these archetypes are common to the unconscious of all humans they constitute a sort of collective inheritance, which he termed the collective unconscious.

THE CONCEPT OF THE ARCHETYPE grew out of the research and personal life experiences of Carl Gustav Jung (1875–1961), a Swiss psychoanalyst who was the anointed heir to Freud's kingdom before their relationship descended into feuding and bitterness, as with so many of Freud's associates (see Adler, page 13). An important bone of contention between the two was Jung's interest in mystical aspects of the psyche, and it is easy to dismiss, as Freud did, archetypes and the collective unconscious as anti-scientific mumbo-jumbo and mere mysticism. But Jung's conception and discussion of archetypes leaves much room for debate. Did he conceive of the collective unconscious as some sort of world mind or psychic astral plane, or is it simply shorthand for hard-wired, innate aspects of human neurology, which evolved early in our evolutionary history and are therefore encoded in our genes?

Jung certainly compared archetypes to instincts. Like instincts, he believed, archetypes are inherited and hard-wired, but where instincts govern behaviour, archetypes govern thoughts, feelings and perceptions: specifically what Jungians describe as 'psychic apprehensions'. Cognitive psychology, the school of psychology that deals with the mind in terms analogous to computer science, postulates mental modules and programmes that filter and process perceptions, experiences and thoughts, and archetypes can be seen in this light. To put it another way, archetypes are like centres of gravity in the psychic universe, attracting and animating related concepts and imagery.

Jung became 'aware' of archetypes partly through his practice, partly through his reading in world literature and cultures, and partly through his own psychic journey. As an analyst he was forcibly struck by the way in which patients he considered relatively simple and uneducated related imagery replete with symbolism from arcane and cross-cultural sources. If they could not have encountered such symbols in their own lives, where could they be coming from? His own experience supplied a telling example: only after a series of dreams in which he saw a four-fold radiating pattern did he discover that this symbol had a name – the mandala – and was a common theme in Eastern cultures. If such concepts had not arisen from personal experience, Jung reasoned, they must be innate, reflecting 'psychic apprehensions' that lay at the root of humanity itself, springing from a shared or collective unconscious.

Jung identified a handful of major archetypes (although he allowed that the total number might be unlimited), including the wise old man and his female counterpart, the *magna mater*, or great mother. Discussing the wise old man, for instance, Jung wrote: 'The wise old man appears in dreams in the guise of a magician, doctor, priest, teacher, professor, grandfather, or any person possessing authority.' Also, there were the self and the shadow, and the anima and animus (the opposing gender aspects of each individual). These and other archetypes can be spotted everywhere from popular culture (e.g. Bugs Bunny as the trickster or Gandalf as the wise old man) to the esoteric (Tarot's Major Arcana cards influenced Jung's thinking, as did the symbolism of alchemy and magic).

AVERSION THERAPY

*A form of psychotherapy where someone is
conditioned to associate specific thoughts and/or
behaviours with negative consequences, supposedly
with the result that the subject becomes 'averse'
(i.e. avoids/dislikes) the target thoughts/behaviours.
A typical example of aversion therapy is
conditioning someone to avoid alcohol by giving
them a drug that makes them sick whenever they
drink alcohol.*

A VERSION THERAPY is a form of behavioural
modification or behaviour therapy, which
works because animals (including humans) have
evolved to learn quickly to avoid dangerous stimuli.
Conditioned food aversion is where an association
between ingesting something and being sick rapidly

leads to a long-lasting and deep-seated aversion (as in the case of someone who gets sick from bad shellfish, and subsequently feels nauseous at the sight, smell or even thought of shellfish).

As a therapy it developed from work on conditioning, such as Pavlov's dogs and the Skinner box (see pages 143 and 177 respectively). For instance, dogs that were trained to associate certain stimuli with electric shocks quickly grew to dislike said stimuli. If such experiments sound cruel, imagine the ethical issues surrounding aversion therapy in humans. Yet such considerations have not stopped aversion therapy from being used from the 1920s to the present day.

SHOCKTAILS

Possibly the first application of aversion therapy was in the treatment of alcohol abuse in 1925, using electric shocks. Ten years later chemical aversion therapy for alcoholism was first tried, and today it is still in use with the drug Antabuse (the proprietary name for disulfuram) prescribed to cause nausea, vomiting and palpitations when alcohol is consumed.

More controversially, aversion therapy was widely used to 'treat' homosexuality, seen as pathological until the late 1960s and beyond. In 1935, for instance, a man was asked to engage in homoerotic fantasies and given electric shocks. A similar experiment from 1963 involved a barefoot man standing on an electrified metal floor and given shocks while being shown pictures of naked men. After 4,000 shocks the subject reportedly became bisexual.

Aversion therapy for homosexuality lurched further into farce in the late 1950s with the development by psychiatrist Kurt Freund of chemical methods. Freund administered apomorphine to cause dangerous and distressing symptoms including nausea and vomiting while showing his victims pictures of naked men. He also developed a device where a band clamped around the penis recorded any engorgement, which was supposed to function as a sort of sexual 'lie detector' to ferret out irrepressible erotic responses. Perhaps inevitably, farce eventually led to tragedy in 1964 when a British man with a heart condition died as the result of chemical aversion therapy for homosexuality, after having been administered vomit-inducing drugs in conjunction with a discussion about homosexuality, followed by a dose of LSD while talking about heterosexual fantasies!

As linguist Hugh Rawson points out, 'From the standpoint of a person who is forced to undergo it, "aversion therapy" is difficult to distinguish from punishment or torture.' Yet despite this, it was still relatively common in parts of the US as late as the mid-1980s, and is probably still practised around the world.

BARNUM EFFECT

The tendency to accept generic statements as accurate personal descriptions, particularly when they are flattering.

ALSO KNOWN AS THE FALLACY of personal validation, the Barnum effect or phenomenon is named for the nineteenth-century US showman and charlatan P. T. Barnum (1810–91), for it incorporates two of his famous dictums: 'My secret of success is always to have a little something for everyone' and 'There's a sucker born every minute'. A typical Barnum-effect statement may be detailed or appear specific, but in fact will be vague, ambiguous and/or self-contradictory and thus applicable to everyone. Whether they are aware of it or not, the phenomenon is a major tool of astrologers, psychics and fortune tellers, alongside cold reading and other tricks (see page 49).

The effect was first demonstrated in 1949 in an experiment by US psychologist Bertram Forer (1914–2000), who gave college students personality profiles supposedly based on a test they had taken earlier. In fact the profiles were composed of statements taken from astrology books, and all the subjects got the same list (see overleaf – number 11 is a particularly good example of a statement that covers all the bases). Asked to 'rate on a scale of zero to five the degree to which the description reveals the basic characteristics of your personality', the subjects gave an average rating of more than four out of five. Forer himself did not mention Barnum; the effect was christened by US psychologist Paul Everett Meehl (1920–2003) in 1956.

Knowing about the Barnum effect is one thing – resisting it is another. Personality psychologists worry about the phenomenon as it threatens to undermine the sometimes shaky credibility of their discipline. Yet the best advice they can offer is to be aware of the effect and try not to give in to flattery.

DO ANY OF THESE SOUND FAMILIAR?

1. You have a great need for other people to like and admire you.
2. You have a tendency to be critical of yourself.
3. You have a great deal of unused capacity which you have not turned to your advantage.
4. While you have some personality weaknesses, you are generally able to compensate for them.
5. Your sexual adjustment has presented problems for you.
6. Disciplined and self-controlled outside, you tend to be worrisome and insecure inside.
7. At times you have serious doubts as to whether you have made the right decision or done the right thing.
8. You prefer a certain amount of change and variety and become dissatisfied when hemmed in by restrictions and limitations.
9. You pride yourself as an independent thinker and do not accept others' statements without satisfactory proof.
10. You have found it unwise to be too frank in revealing yourself to others.
11. At times you are extroverted, affable and sociable, while at other times you are introverted, wary and reserved.
12. Some of your aspirations tend to be pretty unrealistic.
13. Security is one of your major goals in life.

BOBO DOLL

A large inflatable toy, shaped like a ten pin and painted as a clown, with a weighted, round bottom so that it can be punched or kicked over and will bounce back up.

THE BOBO DOLL is famous in the annals of psychological research for featuring in a set of classic experiments by Albert Bandura (b. 1925), in which children apparently showed a tendency to imitate the aggressive behaviours of 'models', whether these were adults in the same room or seen on TV.

Bandura's social-learning theory suggested that many behaviours are learned through imitation of models, especially parents and other significant adults, but also models in the mass media. In 1961, as a professor at Stanford University, he tested this theory with an experiment in which boys and girls aged between three and six years old played with toys in a playroom when an adult came in and started beating up a five-foot Bobo doll. When later given the chance to play with a child-sized, three-foot high version, the children who had observed aggressive 'models' were much more likely to beat up on the Bobo doll themselves. Boys were more likely to be physically aggressive than girls and in general the children imitated male 'models' more. In a later version of the experiment, children who watched a video of a violent 'model' tended to be more aggressive to the Bobo doll.

The Bobo doll experiments are often cited as evidence for the potential impact of violence in TV programmes, films, etc, and also seem to support the theory that children learn how to behave by watching others and imitating or 'modelling' their behaviour accordingly. However, within psychology itself the status of these classic experiments is more contentious. Apart from the ethical issues involved, it is also argued that the Bobo doll experiment had poor construct validity, which is to say that the 'aggressive' behaviour shown by the children was actually more like rough-and-tumble high-jinks, and that they were smiling and laughing – in other words, Bandura's experiments didn't necessarily say that much about aggressive behaviour in the real world. Another way of putting this is that the experiment lacked ecological validity.

Perhaps more serious is the criticism that the behaviour displayed by the children was more the result of the experiment's 'demand characteristics' – that the children were trying to do what they thought the experimenter wanted them to do. Having seen an adult bash the Bobo doll, the children assumed they were supposed to do likewise. Demand characteristics are a major problem area in the design of psychology experiments, and the Bobo doll experiment is a classic illustration. Bobo dolls are still widely available as toys, although today they are better known as 'Bop

Bags', so you could repeat the experiment were it not for the ethical considerations and possibility that it is fundamentally flawed anyway.

BRAINWASHING

Trying radically to change someone's beliefs or attitudes through coercive and insidious physical and psychological methods, such as sensory deprivation, indoctrination, hypnotism, sleep deprivation, abuse and even drugs.

THE TERM MEANS DIFFERENT things in different contexts. Today it refers mainly to the process by which religious cults allegedly force new recruits to cut themselves off from their old lives and utterly embrace a new philosophy or belief system. When the term first appeared in the 1950s and 1960s, however, it was linked to alleged activities of Communists accused of changing the ideology of citizens and particularly American prisoners of war through supposed mind-control techniques.

The term 'brain-washing' was coined in 1950 by journalist Edward Hunter, who went on to write a book about indoctrination practices in communist China, *Brain-washing in Red China: The Calculated Destruction of Men's Minds*. Hunter claimed that the Communist Party used what they called *xi-nao* ('wash-brain') techniques to turn normal citizens into rabid zealots. It later turned out that Hunter was a CIA agent, but whatever his agenda his theories hit the mainstream during the Korean War when American soldiers taken prisoner by the North Korean and Chinese communists were paraded in front of cameras making pro-Communist statements. Even more astonishingly, when the war ended a number of American POWs refused repatriation, apparently preferring to stay in China.

To the American public this was shocking and scary: red-blooded Americans somehow transformed into Commie patsies! Only some form of psychological witchcraft could be responsible – a contemporary commenter noted sarcastically that surely 'nothing less than a combination of the theories of Dr I. P. Pavlov and the wiles of Dr Fu Manchu would produce such results'. Brainwashing became cemented in the popular consciousness with the success of Richard

Condon's 1959 novel *The Manchurian Candidate* and subsequent film adaptations, in which an American POW is brainwashed and sent back to America as a 'sleeper' assassin, who can be turned into a presidential assassin by a simple code word. Another version of brainwashing in the popular consciousness is Stockholm Syndrome (see page 195).

MIND CONTROL

Academic theories about the supposed mechanism of brainwashing focused on both sensory deprivation (SD) and over stimulation, both of which can be used as psychological torture. The Americans took brainwashing claims seriously enough for the CIA to launch MK Ultra, a decades-long covert programme of research into supposed mind-control technology, which resulted in at least one death and the widespread unethical treatment and abuse of unwitting American subjects.

Psychologists have now concluded, however, that there is no such thing as brainwashing. People can be coerced into acting in a certain way, but they cannot be forced against their will to change their underlying belief structure. The American POWs who resisted repatriation, for instance, may have done so out of fear of being court-martialled for collaboration. Unfortunately, the brainwashing myth still bears fruit in the form of deprogramming, a system of abusive practices similar to those supposedly used in brainwashing, in which deprogrammers 'rescue' people deemed to have joined a cult, and attempt effectively to 'reverse brainwash' them. Deprogramming is pseudoscientific and unethical, yet even the *Encyclopaedia Britannica* claims that it 'has proved somewhat successful'. Brainwashing is a powerful meme.

CARPENTERED ENVIRONMENT AND THE MÜLLER-LYER ILLUSION

The illusion consists of two parallel lines, one with outward-pointing arrowheads and the other with inward-pointing ones. The latter line looks longer than the former, but in fact both lines are identical in length. The illusion remains even when you know this.

THE MÜLLER-LYER OR ARROWHEAD illusion is one of the best known and most studied in psychology. First described in 1889 by obscure German psychologist Franz Carl Müller-Lyer (1857–1916), multiple theories have since been advanced to explain the illusion. Perhaps the best known is that of Richard Gregory, who suggested that it was the result of top-down processing. This is where the 'higher' orders of brain function (such as knowledge and beliefs) impose meaning and even form perceptions, effectively moulding and recombining the raw perceptual data. According to this theory, conscious perceptions are constructs that reflect our preconceptions, biases and expectations as much as reality. In the case of the Müller-Lyer perception, Gregory suggested, we unconsciously interpret the diagonals as perspective cues, as if we were looking at the distant corner of a wall (the outward-pointing arrowheads) or the near corner of the outside of a box or building (the inward-pointing arrowheads). The former therefore seems further away and logically must be longer in reality if it covers the same span on the retina.

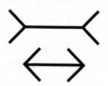

Gregory's theory is somewhat undermined by a version of the illusion that replaces the arrowheads with circles, either right at the tip of the lines or sitting over the ends. The illusion persists, but the circles don't appear to be giving the same perspective cues. On the other hand, Gregory's theory appears to be supported by the intriguing finding that the power of the illusion – and therefore the process of perception itself – may be influenced by culture. According to the 'carpentered world hypothesis', first advanced by South African psychologist William Hudson (b. 1914), the illusion only works on people from cultures with built environments full of artefacts constructed from straight lines and right angles (so-called 'carpentered worlds'). Tribal cultures in sub-Saharan Africa, such as the Zulu and San, lack such 'carpentered' artefacts and so might be expected not to have absorbed the perspective cues apparently at work in the Müller-Lyer illusion. Sure enough, not only do people from such cultures lack two-dimensional representations of three-dimensional objects in their art, they also appear unable to interpret linear perspective in pictures and are relatively resistant to the Müller-Lyer and related illusions. If it is genuine, the carpentered world phenomenon is a potent illustration of the constructive nature of perception.

CLEVER HANS

CLEVER HANS, ALSO KNOWN by the German version, *der kluge Hans*, was a horse that had apparently been trained to understand human speech, do sums and possibly even read minds. Controlled experiments revealed that the horse was responding to non-verbal cues from questioners in such a way as to mimic comprehension, and this type of experimenter effect is now known as the Clever Hans effect or phenomenon.

Hans was trained by retired German mathematics teacher Wilhelm von Osten (1838–1909) in the city of Elberfeld around the turn of the last century. Hans was introduced to the world in 1901 and amazed all-comers by working out quite complex sums (such as square roots), answering by tapping his hooves the required number of times. The horse performed successfully even in von Osten's absence, silencing

sceptics. Theories advanced to explain Hans' feats included high levels of animal intelligence and telepathy. Hans was just one of several 'Elberfeld horses', trained in accordance with the theories of Karl Krall, an eccentric but influential animal psychologist whose theories became popular in Germany. Another of the Elberfeld horses, known as Muhamed, could supposedly extract cube roots, critique music and spell words, while an 'intelligent' dog trained in the Krall mode was later said to philosophize and appreciate literature.

In 1904, however, Hans was investigated by the psychologist Oskar Pfungst (1874–1932), who employed a variety of clever controls. For instance, Pfungst had one person whisper a number in Hans' right ear and a second number was whispered into the left ear by someone else – hence the experimenters themselves had no way of knowing the correct sum of the two numbers. In such conditions Hans was unable to perform, for it turned out that all Hans did was tap his hoof until the questioner unconsciously cued him to stop by means of subtle, non-verbal signals such as changes of stance. Pfungst observed that the questioner could produce cues involuntarily and he even identified the precise mechanism involved: when the questioner had finished posing his question and was ready for Hans to start answering, he shifted forwards and looked down at Hans' hoof. When Hans reached the correct number, the questioner typically straightened up and changed his breathing pattern. Von Osten wore wide-brimmed hats that tended to exaggerate even minor head movements, which probably helped his horses learn to pick up on non-verbal cues.

The Clever Hans effect is of vital importance in studies of animal intelligence and human–animal communication. It continues to plague and confound research into, for instance, the ability of chimpanzees to communicate using sign language. It even plays a controversial role in debates over facilitated communication, a system/therapy for autistic and disabled people who struggle to communicate. In facilitated communication, providing tools such as keyboards, picture boards and synthesizers seems to allow previously non-communicative people to display much higher intelligence and/or language skills than were previously apparent. But controlled studies of facilitated communication suggest that a form of the Clever Hans effect is at work, with facilitators unwittingly controlling/cueing responses. When facilitators are kept 'blind' of the stimuli, the disabled people turn out to be unable to respond appropriately.

Clever Hans-style phenomena, also known as Rosenthal effects, are a major issue in experimental design in general across the sciences. Unless precautions such as double-blind controls (where neither experimenter nor subject is in the know) are taken, experimenters can unconsciously affect outcomes, contaminating results.

COCKTAIL PARTY EFFECT

At a crowded cocktail party you are chatting with someone, seemingly oblivious to the hubbub of voices around you, when you notice your name mentioned by someone on the other side of the room.

HOW IS THIS POSSIBLE? You were focused on the conversation with the person next to you, and not listening to the other conversation, which is no louder than a dozen others going on all around you, yet you became aware of the distant conversation as soon as your name was mentioned. This is known as the cocktail party effect or phenomenon, a term coined in 1957 by the British telecommunications engineer Colin Cherry (1914–79).

The obvious implication is that you *could* hear the other conversation, and that at some level your brain was processing the auditory information involved – i.e. some part of your mind was listening to the other conversation, even though you may not have been consciously aware of it. Since you didn't know which of the many conversations going on would mention your name, you must presumably have been 'listening' to all the conversations at a pre-conscious level of awareness. Interestingly, the effect is much weaker when listening to recorded cocktail party-style conversations. It seems to rely strongly on the stereo nature of binaural (two-eared) hearing, but tone and quality of voice (e.g. whether the voice is male or female) are also important.

The cocktail party effect has important implications for psychological models of perception, attention and consciousness. It suggests, for instance, that there are different levels of consciousness, and that you can be more or less aware of sensory input even when not paying full attention to it. But how much processing is going on below the threshold of conscious awareness? To put it another way, to what extent are we not aware of how much we are aware of?

The cocktail party effect may not be all it's cracked up to be, however. A 2001 study found evidence that the effect may be down to little more than wandering attention. People with high working-memory spans, who are good at maintaining their focus of attention, were much less likely to exhibit the effect than those with low working-memory spans. It seems that the latter group tended quickly to lose focus on the conversation at hand, so that their attention wandered and they had 'half an ear' on other conversations. Accordingly they were much more likely to hear their name when it was mentioned in the background. So rather than the cocktail party effect being proof that we can hear (in the sense of automatically, pre-consciously processing) something without attention, it may simply be evidence that most people are not very good at keeping their attention on one thing.

SENSORY PERCEPTION

There are other phenomena that do seem to prove that high-level processing of sensory input is possible without explicit conscious awareness; most notably blindsight. This is where someone (usually after brain damage) claims not to be able to see something but is nonetheless able to point to it.

COGNITIVE DISSONANCE

Psychological tension arising when someone holds two opposing or clashing cognitions (beliefs, thoughts or knowledge).

COGNITIVE DISSONANCE THEORY was primarily articulated by US psychologist Leon Festinger (1919–89), growing out of his landmark study, *When Prophecy Fails* (1956), an account of what happened to a UFO cult when its doomsday prediction did not come true. The cult believed that a great flood was imminent but that the true believers would be rescued by an alien spaceship. When the Apocalypse failed to materialize, the group then claimed that it had been averted because of their faith, becoming stronger believers than ever. This outcome was predicted by Festinger's theory, which says that when cognitive dissonance (in this case between the belief that the space people were coming and the fact that they didn't) occurs, people change their cognitions to reduce it (in this case by coming up with a rationalisation for the intergalactic no-shows).

Cognitive dissonance is part of a wider theory, which sees the need to achieve cognitive consistency as one of the primary drivers of human psychology, alongside hunger, sex, etc. Dissonance acts as a sort of feedback mechanism to help maintain consistency. When cognitions cause dissonance, the dissonance in turn motivates us to act to reduce the dissonance. This can be done in one of three ways: changing one of the cognitions (possibly by changing 'counter-attitudinal behaviour'), decreasing the perceived importance of dissonant cognitions (i.e. it doesn't matter that I just betrayed my long-held views on X because actually X is a trivial matter), and/or adding further cognitions (such as rationalisations or justifications).

Another prediction that follows from dissonance theory is that people will act to filter and control their cognitions so as to prevent dissonance arising in the first place, for instance by not reading or watching material that might conflict with their established beliefs and prejudices. Thus the theory explains, for instance, why liberals in the US tend to get their news from *The Daily Show* but conservatives only watch Fox.

Cognitive dissonance theory has had a major impact on social psychology, partly because it made predictions that could be tested by experiment and partly because those experiments produced some intriguing and counter-intuitive results. For instance, in a 1959 experiment Festinger and his colleagues showed that the strength of dissonance and resulting cognitive adaptation related to the strength of compliance (the factors forcing the subject into a dissonant state). They got students to do a painfully boring task and then paid them either $1 or $20 to convince another student that it would be fun to do. The subjects who got paid $1 changed their own beliefs about the task, convincing themselves it had been fun; in other words the less they were rewarded, the more ready they were to lie to themselves. This is known as the less-leads-to-more effect, also called the negative incentive effect, and is contrary to traditional reinforcement theory, which posits people as rational actors. Where reinforcement theory says we dislike things that cause us pain, cognitive dissonance theory says we justify our suffering by convincing ourselves that painful things are better. In another form this is known as commodity theory: goods and products are perceived to have more value when there is a cost attached to them.

However, the concept of dissonance has also been criticized as vague and ambiguous. According to one school of thought, dissonance is nothing more than guilt.

COLD READING

Techniques for convincing a stranger that you can 'read' them, using psychic powers, mediumistic communication with spirits or any other form of anomalous information transfer.

THIS TYPE OF READING is labelled as 'cold' because the reader comes to the interaction 'cold', as in without any prior information or research. Hot reading, by contrast, involves research such as previous questioning, detective work or simply googling someone. In both cases the important phenomenon at work is subjective validation, where information supplied by the reader is validated by the subject (aka the sitter) – in other words, the sitter is the one who does all the cognitive work, investing statements with meaning and supplying answers to questions.

'YOU'RE ON THE VERGE OF MAKING A BIG DECISION IN YOUR LIFE . . .'

Basic cold reading need involve no more than producing a string of statements, and leaving the sitter to make connections and find meaning. More advanced cold-reading techniques make use of a range of verbal and non-verbal feedback from the sitter, such as pupil dilation, breathing rate and posture, as well as Sherlock Holmes-style deduction from their personal appearance, clothes, jewellery, accent and mode of speech, etc. The feedback helps the reader to proceed from the general to the specific.

Cold reading is the primary device used by psychics, mediums and mentalists. Not all of them use cold reading cynically or even consciously – there may be many psychics, for instance, who believe in their own gifts and are unaware that they are using cold reading (such cases are known as pious frauds).

Typically, cold reading starts with 'fishing' statements, for example, 'Is the name "Michael" significant?' – allowing audience members to self-select or prompting sitters to start providing feedback. Cold readers also make use of the Barnum effect, making general and widely applicable statements. Advanced cold readers may use surveys and research statistics to maximize the likely applicability of their statements.

Once a sitter or audience member subjectively validates a fishing statement or question, the reader feeds back the information as a statement, allowing them to claim credit for it. Cold readers make many guesses and ask many questions – only a few need to garner 'hits' because of the selective-memory effect. Sitters will only remember the hits, forgetting all the misses. Cold reading is often assisted by the fact that sitters are highly motivated to find meaning and attribute significance, but just as Barnum-style statements work without any contact between author and audience, a cold reading requires no actual interaction between reader and sitter.

Cold reading is also a useful tool for salespeople, and an important factor for other professions to consider. For instance, it is likely that criminal profiles, Rorschach ink-blot readings and personality inventory tests all work on similar principles of subjective validation and selective memory.

CULTURE-BOUND SYNDROMES

Psychiatric disorders specific to particular cultures, often with no direct equivalent in the West.

SOME MAY BE VARIANTS of what is known today as mass psychogenic disorder (and used to be labelled mass hysteria); some may be culture-specific forms taken by disorders such as schizophrenia; others may be culturally inflected mechanisms for coping with stress. Because culture-bound syndromes (CBSs) reflect indigenous beliefs and superstitions, they seem exotic, strange and sometimes ridiculous to us, but this reflects an ethnocentric viewpoint.

So far, so exotic, but CBS as a category is not clear-cut. Should it include other forms of mass psychogenic illness, such as witch-hunting panics and other social phobias (for instance, fears in Central American countries that Americans are kidnapping people for their organs, or in South Africa that witch-like prostitutes are hypnotizing men and stealing their semen)? If so, should it extend to social panics in the West, such as bogus social workers and satanic ritual abuse? Some psychiatric diseases, such as anorexia, seem to be confined to Western cultures: do they count as CBSs? Meanwhile in some cultural contexts, behaviour and beliefs that would be characterized as deviant or dysfunctional in the West may seem rational or normal, or make sense as a social coping mechanism. CBSs help to illustrate that in some senses psychiatric illness should be defined simply as deviation from a local norm.

EXOTIC SYNDROMES

There are dozens of CBSs, and the same syndrome may have different names in different languages. Among the best-known examples are *koro*, *amok* and *windigo*. *Koro* is the Malay language name for penis-stealing panic, which is surprisingly widespread around the world. *Koro* is marked by fear that some form of witchcraft can lead to shrinking or disappearance of a man's penis or woman's ▶

breasts and/or vulva. A single case can lead to a country-wide panic, which in turn can spark off witch hunts that lead to fatal vigilante action. In 1997, for instance, penis-stealing panic spread across West Africa from Cameroon to the Ivory Coast, leading to the murder of at least sixty suspected 'sorcerers' at the hands of lynch mobs. In the Far East *koro* is found from China to Indonesia, and can lead to self-mutilation as sufferers attempt to clamp or pin their penises to prevent them shrinking into the body.

Amok is a Malaysian CBS, although it has been reported from Polynesia to Puerto Rico, characterized by a period of intense brooding followed by outbursts of uncontrolled aggression – hence *running amok*. *Wendigo* is a strange form of psychosis that traditionally affected Native American tribes around the Great Lakes, especially in winter, in which men would lose their appetite and suffer nausea, followed by delusions of possession by a cannibalistic spirit monster called the *wendigo*.

Other CBSs include *taijin kyofusho*, a Japanese disorder characterized by anxiety that one's personal body and body functions are repugnant and embarrassing; ghost sickness, a Native American syndrome characterized by fear of death, anxiety and panic attacks, traditionally blamed on witchcraft; and *pa-leng*, a Chinese and south-east Asian fear that coldness and wind can cause impotence, sickness and death.

DEFENCE MECHANISM

An unconscious pattern of thought or behaviour that protects the conscious mind from thoughts and feelings that cause anxiety or discomfort.

ALTHOUGH INITIALLY A TERM in psychoanalysis, defence mechanisms are widely recognized by psychotherapy in general. The term originated with Freud, who described defence mechanisms as ways in which the ego (the conscious self) protects itself against the id (the unconscious repository of base urges and illicit drives and desires). Defence mechanisms could be described as a form of repression, and as strategies to combat cognitive dissonance (see page 45). Freud suggested that maladaptive defence mechanisms can turn into neuroses.

FROM DENIAL TO SUBLIMATION

Freud and particularly his daughter Anna (1895–1982), in her book *The Ego and the Mechanisms of Defence* (1936), described and explored a great many types of defence mechanism, and several of them are common currency in psychotherapy and popular culture in general:

- Denial: the most straightforward strategy when faced with an uncomfortable feeling or truth is to deny it, such as when a jilted lover acts as if the relationship never ended.
- Rationalization: coming up with after-the-fact justification for actions or cognitions, such as a drug cheat who claims he had to do it because everyone else did so.
- Projection: projecting negative or difficult feelings about oneself onto others, such as when a bully accuses her victim of being the bully.
- Repression: in psychoanalysis, when problematic feelings or thoughts are banished to the unconscious. In a sense, all defence mechanisms are forms of repression.
- Displacement: taking problematic feelings about one situation and transferring them into another, substitute situation, such as taking out work stress on your family. In psychoanalysis, someone might displace their Oedipal feelings by marrying a girl just like mother.

- Regression: reverting to behaviour or thinking from an earlier stage in development, typically childhood, when life was simpler and less problematic. For instance, when you react to criticism by having a tantrum or cope with anxiety by cuddling up with an old toy.
- Sublimation: channelling psychic tension into more acceptable outlets. For instance, Freud theorized that the painter Cezanne owed his creative energy to his sublimated sexual desire. Similar theories have been advanced about Isaac Newton.

DÉJÀ VU

*The illusion of having previously experienced
something that is actually being experienced for the
first time, déjà vu is French for 'already seen'.*

IT IS EXTREMELY COMMON, experienced by up to 80
per cent of people between 20–25 years old, and less
commonly with increasing age. Other variants include
déjà entendu (already heard), *déjà éprouvé* (already
experienced or tested), *déjà fait* (already done), *déjà
pensé* (already thought), *déjà raconté* (already told or
recounted), *déjà voulu* (already desired) and *déjà vécu*
(already lived). This last variant is perhaps the more
accurate description of the majority of déjà vu cases,
where it is not just the visual aspect that seems familiar.

Déjà vu is generally distinguished by a sense of
otherworldliness to the episode, although it is not clear

whether this is an integral component of the illusion/ delusion, or simply the consequence of knowing that what you are feeling must be illusory. The illusion may be so convincing that you feel you can predict what is about to happen or be said, although there is no record of anyone actually having done so.

FROM BEYOND THE GRAVE

Alternatively, déjà vu can be seen as evidence for the paranormal. The experiencer may be remembering something, but something from a past life; in other words, déjà vu is evidence of reincarnation. Or you could be picking up on someone else's memory, through telepathy, or have experienced a scene without ever having been there, through some sort of clairaudience. None of these, however, account for the feeling that the event is so familiar you know what is coming next, which suggests that a form of precognition (the ability to know the future) is involved.

Explanations for déjà vu depend on whether you believe the experiencer really *has* already seen/ experienced the event/scene. If so, then what needs explaining is the 'first' experience, while the déjà vu itself is simply a form of remembering. It could be that the person with déjà vu has indeed already visited a place/met someone, but cannot remember it, a phenomenon known as paramnesia. In psychoanalysis paramnesia can be a defence mechanism, indicative that the original occurrence was the cause of distress and hence has been repressed.

Déjà vu is a symptom experienced by sufferers of temporal-lobe epilepsy, sometimes signalling the onset of a seizure. This suggests that the phenomenon has a neurological cause – in other words, it is indeed an illusion, and there is no prior memory causing the sensation. In epileptics the explanation would seem to be that an anomalous discharge in the temporal lobe creates the illusion of prior memory and/or the overwhelming sensation of familiarity. Something similar may be at work in the general population, related to erroneous activation of the 'familiarity' centres.

An alternative neurological explanation is that somehow different parts of the brain become desynchronized (e.g. there is momentary disruption of communication between the two hemispheres of the brain), causing 'splitting' of a perception. Thus the brain processes the same experience twice, possibly with a microsecond time lag between the two, and this could account for the unsettling déjà vu.

Finally, a purely psychological explanation, known as restricted paramnesia, is that the new experience is indeed similar to an actual memory, but one which has been so altered by recurrent reconstruction and elaboration that it triggers a false match.

Less common but still widespread is the opposite of déjà vu: *jamais vu*. This is where someone is unable to recognize something that should be familiar, such as walking into your own house but not recognizing it. Pathological forms of *jamais vu* characterize conditions such as prosopagnosia, the inability to recognize faces, usually associated with brain damage.

DELUSIONS

A fixed belief that does not make sense given the available evidence, is at odds with the cultural norm, and is resistant to all reason.

DEPENDING ON YOUR POLITICS, everything from climate-change denial to communism could be characterized and/or derided as a delusion, but in a psychiatric sense delusions are peculiar and often disabling ideas at odds with external reality. Delusions are one of the characteristic symptoms of schizophrenia, and are also found in dementia, brain damage and other conditions. They come in many weird and terrible varieties, but the most common in schizophrenia are delusions of persecution, delusions of reference and delusions of control.

FORMS OF DELUSION

- Delusions of persecution involve the conviction that people are 'out to get you', with the focus of the delusion ranging from a plotting neighbour to a global conspiracy. Such delusions are experienced by 65 per cent of schizophrenics, according to a large-scale survey taken in 1974. Delusions of reference involve the conviction that completely unrelated remarks and references, whether from the media or overheard conversations, relate to you, usually in some negative fashion. Delusions of control involve the conviction that your actions, emotions and even thoughts are not under your control, but are being controlled by someone else or some external force, whether space aliens, powerful government agencies, devils, etc.

- Other types of delusion include delusions of grandeur (believing you have special abilities, qualities or status); hypochondriacal delusions, where you falsely believe you have some illness; nihilistic delusions, where you believe you don't exist or are worth nothing (common in depression); and delusional jealousy, where you believe that someone close to you is persistently unfaithful with everyone.

- Cotard's syndrome is marked by the delusion that parts of your body are rotting or that you have died, apparently combining hypochondriacal delusions with delusions of depersonalization. Erotomania, also ▶

known as de Clérambault's syndrome, is where you develop the delusion that someone else – usually an authority figure/celebrity – is secretly in love with you and is constantly sending subtle signals to that effect, despite explicit denials. The Mignon delusion is a common childhood fantasy that your 'real' parents are rich/famous/illustrious and will eventually reclaim you. Fregoli syndrome, named for a famous quick-change artist, is the delusion that multiple different people are actually the same person, who is constantly changing his disguise or appearance. Capgras syndrome is a frightening and tragic condition marked by the delusion that one or more loved ones have been replaced by impostors who look exactly the same.

- Delusions can be categorized as monothematic or polythematic. Monothematic delusions have a single theme, such as the delusions of misidentification in Capgras syndrome. Polythematic delusions cover a range of subjects, as in schizophrenics who believe that a global conspiracy against them includes mind-control technology and subliminal messages in the media. Delusions can be bound up together as fully fledged delusional systems.

One theory advanced to explain delusions is that they are an attempt to make sense of disordered perceptions. For example, in Capgras syndrome it may be that while the part of the brain responsible for identifying faces functions normally, the part that assigns feelings of familiarity is malfunctioning. Perhaps in order to explain how they can recognize someone but find them unfamiliar, the sufferer develops the delusion that the person has been replaced. Delusions of control may have a similar basis, in that they could be caused by disruption of the normal experience of conscious volition and initiation that accompanies normal actions and thoughts (which in turn explains the striking observation that sufferers can tickle themselves). If you say something but don't experience the process of deciding to say it, perhaps the logical conclusion is that an external force is controlling you.

However, explaining delusions as arising from anomalous experience in this fashion fails to explain why delusions are so resistant to logic and cannot be altered or dispelled. Clearly people with delusions must be suffering from some impairment of the ability to evaluate beliefs, perhaps linked to problems with a specific brain region, such as the right frontal lobe.

DISSOCIATION AND FUGUE

Dissociation in a psychological sense is a disconnect between things that are usually associated, such as intentions and actions, events and emotional responses, thoughts and speech, and even between mind and body.

FUNCTIONS AND ASPECTS OF MIND that are normally integrated, such as memory, consciousness and sense of identity, can become dissociated. Ranging from the mild to the severe, examples include driving automatically while thinking about something completely different; feeling nothing in response to an event or memory that ought to provoke sadness or shock; feeling that you are not in control of your actions and you are watching life and yourself from a distance, as if watching a movie; and even forgetting who you are and where you come from. Dissociative disorders can be strange and intriguing, with unsettling implications for consciousness and identity.

Dissociation is a common response to physical and mental trauma or stress, presumably acting as a defence mechanism to protect the self/psyche from unbearable feelings. Approximately seventy-three per cent of people who have a traumatic incident will experience dissociative states during the incident or in the days and weeks that follow. For instance, someone with post-traumatic stress disorder who attends the funeral of a loved one might find that they do not feel grief: they are dissociated from their normal emotional response. Studies estimate that two to ten per cent of the population experience dissociative disorders.

The strangest and most severe dissociative disorders are psychogenic amnesia, fugue and dissociative identity disorder (DID). Psychogenic amnesia is amnesia with no organic (i.e. physical/physiological) cause, brought on by psychological factors such as stress and emotional trauma. This is the sort of amnesia that you see in films such as Hitchcock's *Spellbound*. Its most extreme form is the state known as fugue, from the Latin for 'flight', in which the sufferer not only loses memory for his past life and identity, but will travel some distance and set up a new life under a new identity. There is still considerable doubt as to whether psychogenic amnesia, and fugue states in particular, is 'genuine' or a form of malingering. For instance, take the case of a man facing bankruptcy whose marriage is also in trouble, who goes into a fugue state, moves to another town and starts a new life under an assumed identity. Is the memory loss genuine, or just an elaborate way of ducking responsibilities?

Even more contentious and controversial is DID, which used to be known as multiple personality disorder (MPD). There was a great vogue for MPD in the early years of psychiatry in late Victorian times, with celebrated cases such as Morton Prince's treatment of Sally Beauchamp, the subject of a bestselling 1908 book, *The Dissociation of a Personality*. MPD seemed to prove that there was no unity of consciousness (i.e. no single self), but a number of different streams of consciousness that could dissociate into distinct personalities under pressure. MPD went out of fashion with the supremacy of Freudian psychoanalysis, which suggested that traumatic psychic pressure resulted in repression into the unconscious, rather than separate consciousnesses, but interest resumed in the 1970s. DID is most commonly found in people who have suffered chronic sexual and physical abuse, especially as children. To cope with the pain and fear, new personalities are created or split off.

Proponents of DID point to amazing evidence, such as different personalities needing different spectacle prescriptions and having different allergies, but critics say that DID may be iatrogenic (created by doctors). 'Mythomanic' patients may be confabulating new personalities to meet what they perceive as the demands/wishes of the therapist, especially under the highly suggestible conditions of hypnosis, which is often used as a tool to investigate DID.

But what if DID and fugue are genuine? The legal and philosophical ramifications of extreme dissociative disorders are huge. For instance, who is responsible for a crime committed by one of multiple personalities? Is it fair to punish all the personalities through incarceration of the body they share? Does someone with DID have more than one soul?

DREAMS

Images and thoughts experienced during sleep, often occurring in an apparently meaningful sequence, and usually involving emotions.

DREAMS WERE A GREAT MYSTERY to the ancients, who believed they were messages from the gods or the wanderings of the spirit. Today, although we know a little more about dreams they remain a great mystery.

Contrary to popular belief, children under the age of ten do not have a rich dream life, but adults can expect to have four to six dreams a night, lasting from five to thirty minutes each. The vast majority are not remembered. Most dreams happen during a phase of sleep known as rapid eye movement (REM) sleep, during which the body is mostly paralysed but the mind is almost as active as when you are awake.

Dream content can vary enormously, but the most common dreams involve strong emotions – mostly negative ones, such as fear and anxiety. The most common dream theme is being chased or followed, and dreams usually feature the dreamer as him/herself, along with other known/familiar people.

These facts suggest some explanations for dreaming while appearing to rule out others. For instance, REM sleep is 'expensive' in terms of energy use, so there must be a good reason for dreaming to occur, or evolution would have weeded it out. But what function could dreams serve?

Dreams are of central importance to the theories and practice of psychoanalysis. Freud wrote that 'The interpretation of dreams is the royal road to a knowledge of the unconscious activities of the mind', while Jung believed that dreams gave access to the archetypes of the collective unconscious (see page 16). According to psychoanalysts, dreams rehearse repressed desires and unfulfilled wishes, helping the conscious self or ego deal with the problematic content of the unconscious. If this is true, however, why do we forget around ninety-nine per cent of our dreams? Wouldn't it be more helpful to remember them?

Another explanation is that dreams evolved as a form of simulator, allowing us to rehearse survival strategies in a sort of virtual-reality environment. This might help explain why negative emotions and pursuits are so common in dreams: they help us rehearse coping with dangerous and stressful situations.

EGO, SUPEREGO AND ID

*From the Latin for 'the I, the super-I and the it',
the ego, superego and id make up Freud's tripartite
(three-part) structure of personality, also known as
the structural hypothesis/model/theory.*

A T FIRST FREUD HAD DIVIDED the mind up according
to its topography (which is to say, the layout of
mental space), with the unconscious, preconscious
and conscious. But in 1920, with his structure of
personality, Freud articulated not only a model of
personality but also an account of its development.

The id is the part of the mind that contains the
inherited, biological, 'animal' instincts (which Freud
said included Eros, the sex/life instinct, including the
libido, and Thanatos, the death instinct, responsible
for aggression). It is motivated by the pleasure

principle, which demands instant gratification, from which it derives pleasure, and when it is thwarted it experiences un-pleasure, or pain. The id is not affected by logic or reality, taking no account of the external world. A newborn child is all id.

As the child matures the demands of the id come into constant conflict with the realities of the external world, and the part that has to deal with reality becomes the ego. The ego works on the reality principle, which involves working out how realistically to meet the demands of the id, delaying or compromising gratification in order to achieve pleasure and avoid pain. The ego is rational but without morality or ethics it is purely practical.

Morality comes into the picture via the superego, which absorbs the values and morals of the family and wider society and works to control the impulses of the id, especially those which are taboo, such as lust and aggression. The superego includes the conscience, which punishes the ego with guilt when it transgresses the moral rules or gives in to the id, and the ideal self, which combines the aspirations and ambitions set out for the individual by family and society. Failure of the ego to live up to the ideal self also leads to guilt, but 'proper' behaviour can be rewarded with pride. An overbearing superego and especially an unrealistic ideal self can cause neurosis, anxiety and depression. In the adult, the id is entirely unconscious, while the supergo and the ego extend from the conscious down into the unconscious.

The whole system is supposed to be self-correcting, working via feedback loops based on the principle of tension reduction – seeking the path of thought and behaviour that gives rise to the least psychic tension. Freud himself used the analogy of a horse and a rider for the id and the ego, and given the rather gloomy narrative of tensions, drives and motivations offered by Freud, it is tempting to extend the analogy and imagine a hapless rider clinging onto a careering horse, maddened by lust and greed and kept in check only by the sting of the spur and the whip.

'The poor ego,' wrote Freud in 1932, 'has to serve three harsh masters, and it has to do its best to reconcile demands of all three . . . The three tyrants are the external world, the superego, and the id'.

Perhaps in reaction to this jaded view of human nature, Freud's daughter and other successors developed a more humane spin on his model of the self, in the form of ego psychology. Ego psychology argued that the ego was not defined by its constant internal battle with the id and superego, was not

LOST IN TRANSLATION

The Latin-based/common-usage terms 'ego' and 'id' point to a recurring issue with the translation of Freud's work. Freud himself, for all that he was concerned for psychoanalysis to be taken seriously as a science, for the most part avoided technical jargon and obscurantism. His English translator, James Strachey, however, often chose terms that sounded more technical, perhaps partly to increase their 'scientific' authoritativeness. Ego and id are classic examples; in the original German, Freud calls them simply *das Ich und das Es*, the 'I' and the 'it'.

governed solely by the need to reduce tension, and could be motivated by positive feedback loops such as seeking novelty and mastering new skills.

ELECTROCONVULSIVE THERAPY

*Also known as shock therapy or electric shock
therapy, electroconvulsive therapy (ECT) involves
stimulation of seizures or convulsions similar to
those experienced by grand mal epileptics, by means
of applying an electrical current across the head.*

IN MODERN ECT, A pair of electrodes, which look
a bit like headphones, is fitted over the temples
and a weak electric current (20–30 mA) is applied,
triggering a seizure. Light general anaesthetic and
muscle relaxants have already been administered, so
the seizure does not actually involve convulsions. In
the early days of ECT before anaesthesia and relaxants
were used, convulsions could lead to broken bones
and other injuries. A course of treatment typically
involves six to twelve shocks over a number of weeks,

with side effects including disruption of heart rate, headaches and memory loss.

One of many points of uncertainty and contention about ECT regards the inspiration for its first use by Italian neurologist Ugo Cerletti (1877–1963) in 1938. According to one account, Cerletti got the idea from watching pigs being anaesthetized by electric shock before being butchered, while according to another account he believed (erroneously) that epilepsy and schizophrenia did not occur together, and hence inferred some anti-psychotic effect of seizures. A third version is that Cerletti was aware of an observation that people with epilepsy and depression displayed improvements in mood after a seizure, and again inferred that seizures themselves could have some therapeutic effect. Whatever the initial inspiration, it became apparent that ECT did indeed produce rapid improvements in mood, even in suicidally depressed patients.

ECT is not the only form of shock therapy – the drugs insulin and Metrazol have also been used to trigger seizures, but these methods had lower success rates and are more dangerous than ECT and are no longer used.

SHOCK HORROR

ECT is a controversial treatment, which has had a bad press since the days when it was applied without anaesthetic, and as a result of its alleged use in some institutions as a threat and punishment to keep difficult patients in line. Controversy extends to the clinical evaluation of ECT – doctors and psychiatrists disagree fiercely over how safe it is, when it should be used and even whether it works at all. Some studies show that, in the treatment of very severe depression and schizophrenic catatonia, ECT is more effective with fewer harmful side effects compared to drugs. Other studies, however, seem to show little benefit over placebo treatments, and potentially very severe, long-term damage to memory and brain function.

Perhaps the biggest problem with ECT is that even if you accept that it does work, no one knows how or why. It seems that it is not the shocks themselves that are therapeutic, but the seizures induced. Seizures appear to affect levels of neurotransmitters (chemicals that pass signals between nerve cells) in the brain, boosting some and increasing the effect of others. It may also be that seizures cause the brain to release natural opium-like painkillers called enkephalins, which may account for the mood-boosting effects of ECT.

EMOTIONAL INTELLIGENCE AND EQ

Emotional intelligence (EI) is seen either as a subset of intelligence in general, or as a parallel system of mental abilities alongside rational intelligence (aka 'book smarts').

SINCE THE SUCCESS of Daniel Goleman's 1995 book *Emotional Intelligence*, EI has been a hot topic both in psychology and in the wider world, especially because of its applied nature. EI seems to play at least as big a part as general intelligence in terms of managing and being successful at your career, relationships and life.

The concept of EI predates Goleman. An appreciation of emotion as a core cognitive competence – which is to say, a mental skill/ability that helps us to function better or, in the case of animals, survive – goes back to Darwin.

In 1920 American psychologist E. L. Thorndike wrote about social intelligence, while in the 1970s Howard Gardner's theory of multiple intelligences included inter- and intrapersonal intelligence. Peter Salovey and John D. Myer introduced the term EI in the modern sense in 1990.

There are several different models or theories of EI, but all stress a kind of hierarchy, with basic skills or 'competencies' such as being able to recognize emotion in yourself and others; being able to regulate and manage emotions in yourself and in your relationships with others; and being able to put your emotional skills to work in a variety of ways, such as problem solving or adapting to change. The definition of EI has even been extended to include aspects as varied as morality, persistence and enthusiasm.

But amidst these competing models with their multitude of competencies and attributes there is considerable confusion. Partly this could be down to confusion between two types of EI and the two ways used to measure them. Measurements of EI are sometimes labelled as Emotional Quotient or EQ, to stand alongside IQ. But because emotions are mostly subjective, most measurements of EQ have been done using self-report questionnaires, which don't meet the same objective criteria as IQ tests (composed of questions with right or wrong answers). Accordingly, EI researchers K. V. Petrides and Adrian Furnham suggest that most EQ tests are actually measuring what they call 'trait EI', which describes the role of EI in personality. Also available are IQ-style tests that are supposed to measure 'ability EI', which describes the role of EI in cognition (thinking and reasoning).

A key question in the EI field is the extent to which people can boost their EQ. There are lots of programmes – particularly in the business world – that claim to teach EI skills and boost EQ. Whether this is really possible is an open question; perhaps it is necessary to focus more on 'emotional education' from an early age to improve 'emotional knowledge', to complement the more traditional version of knowledge.

ERIKSON AND THE EIGHT AGES OF MAN

ERIK ERIKSON (1902–1994) IS one of the most significant figures in post-Freudian psychoanalysis. His 'psychosocial theory', popularly known as the eight ages of man, has had a profound and enduring influence on both psychology and wider popular culture.

Erikson went to art school and worked as a teacher before falling into the orbit of the Freud family and the Vienna Psychoanalytic Institute. He was particularly interested in child development, but what marks out his best-known contribution to psychology, his psychosocial theory, is its emphasis on the whole life cycle.

With others, Erikson developed ego psychology, a more positive view of the structure and function of the psyche than Freud's version (see page 92).

THE EIGHT STAGES OF MAN

The theory sets out what Erikson called the development crises facing an individual at certain stages in life from childhood to old age. At each stage a person must resolve a conflict between opposing forces or drives, and either acquire specific 'ego virtues' or suffer psychic damage as a result. The stages are:

- basic trust versus basic mistrust, in early infancy; successful resolution leads to hope
- autonomy versus shame and doubt, in later infancy; leading to will
- initiative versus guilt, in early childhood (preschool); leading to purpose
- industry versus inferiority, in middle childhood; leading to competence
- identity versus role confusion, in puberty and adolescence; leading to fidelity
- intimacy versus isolation, in young adulthood; leading to love
- generativity versus stagnation, in mature adulthood; leading to care
- ego integrity versus despair, in late adulthood; leading to wisdom.

Ego psychology stressed the capacity of the ego for autonomous action, and the role of interaction between the individual and the environment/society in shaping human psychology. His psychosocial theory was more humanistic still, viewing the conflicts facing the ego as opportunities for change and growth, as well as potentially dangerous crises.

Some of the concepts Erikson introduced around this scheme have become common currency in popular culture, particularly the identity crisis experienced by adolescents figuring out their role in life. Others deserve to be better known, for instance, the 'psychosocial moratorium', a sort of time out from progress through the stages during which a person keeps a fluid identity, such as when a young person takes a year out after university to travel before slotting into the more constrained route of career and family.

Erikson anticipated a number of modern concerns that keep his theories contemporary and valid. He described his model as epigenetic, meaning that while the sequence of development was preprogrammed by our biology (i.e. our genes), progress through the sequence depended on the interaction between our biology and our environment. In stressing the continuous nature of development throughout life he offered a more forward-looking model of human psychology, and thus a more hopeful approach than

Freud's gloomy mire of unconscious complexes fixed in the inaccessible and immutable past. In fact Erikson has been criticized for his perceived overoptimism, as well as for the subjective anecdotal nature of his evidence.

FALSE MEMORY

A false memory is either a distorted recollection or an entirely imaginary one.

FALSE MEMORY IS SURPRISINGLY COMMON. The typical analogy between encoding of memory and filing away a document, and particularly between recall and retrieval of a document from a filing cabinet, a book from a library or webpage from the internet, is misleading. Memory is a reconstructive and sometimes purely constructive process. In a sense, all memories are false in that they are not objective duplicates of events and experiences.

False memories can be created in a number of ways. When a memory is reconstructed from incomplete memory fragments, vital elements of the memory can be transposed or introduced. For instance, you might remember a conversation but get the speakers the wrong way round. In one notorious incident a woman who was raped accused memory expert Donald Thompson of being responsible because she had seen him interviewed live on television just before the rape. Memories can also be entirely confabulated, and they can be introduced through suggestion, particularly in impressionable states like hypnosis, or in highly suggestible individuals such as young children and fantasy-prone personalities. All of these processes can be triggered and guided through questioning, hypnosis and the like.

False memory can be experimentally induced, in fact it is extremely easy. One classic experiment revealed the misinformation effect, which is where misinformation supplied to someone becomes incorporated into their recall. Two groups were shown a video of a traffic incident, and one of the groups was given misinformation in the form of a leading question: 'Did you see the red car pass the white one when it was waiting at the stop sign?' There had been no stop sign, but many subjects falsely remembered one. Providing misinformation has been shown to make people half as accurate as they would have been without it, and post-event misinformation has introduced false memories varying from a clean-shaven man having a moustache, to the presence of a large barn in a photo of an empty country landscape.

Other experiments have proved that false memories for entire scenes and traumatic events can be implanted in people's minds. One study convinced people they could recall being lost in a shopping mall as children, while another implanted memories of being attacked by an animal. The classic example from psychology is the false-kidnapping memory of child development pioneer Jean Piaget. As a very young child his nurse claimed to have beaten off an attempt to kidnap him, and he could recall the incident in some detail. She later admitted it had never happened.

Extreme cases such as this are known as false memory syndrome (FMS), a phenomenon which has had serious and sometimes tragic clinical, legal and social consequences. Leading interview techniques and the use of hypnotic memory recovery has led to wholescale confabulation of memories for childhood sex abuse, satanic ritual abuse and alien abduction. FMS is primarily to blame for the entire alien abductee phenomenon, and for sex-abuse panics that have destroyed families and homes.

PAST LIFE REGRESSION

FMS is also probably the explanation for past life regression, which is where someone under hypnosis claims to remember detailed scenes and events from a past life. Past life regression became famous thanks to the success of the 1956 book *The Search for Bridey Murphy* by Morey Bernstein, which detailed how the hypnosis of Virginia Tighe 'recovered' memories of a past life as a poor Irish woman in the nineteenth century, complete with apparently authentic stories, songs and biographical details. Newspapers later discovered that there was no record of any such woman in Ireland, but that Tighe had lived opposite a Bridey Murphy as a child. Her past life 'memories' were the result of paramnesia and hypnotic suggestion colliding to produce FMS.

FREUD

REGARDED BY MANY AS the greatest thinker in psychology and perhaps the pre-eminent genius of the twentieth century, Sigmund Freud (1856–1939) is also damned as a pseudoscientist and false prophet. Paradoxically his status and that of his theories is higher outside of psychology than within.

Freud was an Austrian Jew who trained as a doctor, specialized in neurology and published research in neurobiology. He also narrowly missed out on discovering the anaesthetic properties of cocaine, but succeeded in becoming addicted for a period. Anti-Semitism limited his job opportunities and directed him into psychiatry, and he trained with leading figures such as Jean-Martin Charcot in Paris and Josef Breuer in Vienna. Their reliance on hypnosis, and Breuer's emphasis on hypnotic revelation of suppressed thoughts and emotions, helped lead Freud to formulate a psychological theory of personality disorders, and of personality itself.

Turning away from hypnosis, Freud looked to free association and dream interpretation as the tools with which to unlock the secrets of the unconscious, creating the first fully realized 'talking cure' for psychological problems. With the data he gathered using these tools, Freud formulated a revolutionary theory of personality and psychological function, in which all neuroses and psychoses had their roots in sexual repression. Most shocking of all, he came to the conclusion that this sexual repression was located in early childhood. In particular, Freud concluded, the formation of the personality (consisting of the ego, superego and id – see page 73) and the basis of both normal and maladaptive personality development lay in the Oedipal conflict and its corollaries, castration anxiety and penis envy (see page 148).

In a series of influential and controversial books including *The Interpretation of Dreams* (1900) and *Three Contributions to the Theory of Sex* (1906), Freud created psychoanalysis, both a new philosophy of psychology and a therapeutic method. The scope of psychoanalysis is universal; Freud himself used it to explain everything from the origins of neurosis and the nature of jokes, to religion, culture and anthropology. In a psychoanalytic world everything has meaning, nothing is accidental (see Freudian Slips, page 96).

Though widely condemned at first, the power of Freud's theories proved irresistible, blazing across Europe and conquering American psychotherapy after WWII. Psychoanalysis became synonymous with psychotherapy and had great influence in art, anthropology, the social sciences, history and literary theory.

Since the 1960s, however, Freud has been criticized as a pseudoscientist and his theories damned as unfalsifiable and baseless. Freud's background was in science, and he was keen for psychoanalysis to have proper scientific footing and status, yet in practice he relied on purely subjective and anecdotal sources for his evidence. He claimed that complexes of memory formed in early childhood were responsible for the entire psychic mechanism, but infants lack the brain structures needed to form such memories. Psychoanalysis cannot make testable predictions and cannot be falsified by evidence or experiments, two essential characteristics of true science. In fact Freud dismissed rejection or criticism of his theories as resistance, an example of a defence mechanism, so that any attempt to falsify his ideas paradoxically became confirmation of them.

More specifically, some key aspects of psychoanalytic theory are today regarded as unpalatable and regressive. For instance, Freud argued that women were defined by their penis envy – i.e. by their deficiency – and that because they could not have a proper Oedipal conflict their moral development must be inferior to that of men.

Despite the pseudoscientific nature of Freudian psychoanalysis and evidence casting doubt on its therapeutic value, psychoanalysis continues to be practised, popular and influential. Much of Freud, especially his concept of the unconscious, has become deeply embedded in modern thinking and popular culture, to the point where psychoanalysis is arguably as integral to our world view as science.

FREUDIAN SLIPS

A Freudian slip is a mistake with hidden significance:
a meaningful slip of the tongue, although there
can also be Freudian slips of the pen and lapses of
memory.

WHAT MAKES A FREUDIAN SLIP special and different from a simple mistake is that although the slip may be unintentional it is not random – at least, not according to Freud and the psychoanalytic school of thought. Freud believed that the unconscious mind is a seething mass of thoughts and emotions too dangerous, shameful and transgressive to be allowed to roam free in the buttoned-up world of the conscious mind. Like an iceberg, the vast bulk of the human personality exists below the surface, and although it is not 'visible' in the sense of being consciously accessible, its gravity and inertia influence and even control the conscious mind. A simple and apparently trivial mis-speaking – what Freud called a *fehlleistung* (a German word with no direct translation, see below) – can be a window onto the lightless region of the unconscious, revealing this mechanism of control.

In modern psychoanalysis the technical term for a Freudian slip is parapraxis, a word coined from Greek roots by James Strachey, the influential translator of the standard English edition of Freud's writings. Critics have complained that by using pseudoscientific jargon Strachey actually lost much of the flavour and style of Freud's original language.

In fact, critics have problems with the entire concept of parapraxis, at least as Freud understood it. Freud insisted that almost any slip of the tongue is indicative of unconscious complexes at work, but modern psychologists say he massively overinterpreted simple cognitive glitches. So much of our mental processing is automatic and pre-conscious that it would be surprising if meaningless errors did *not* creep in; for instance, mistakenly saying words or sounds that seem more natural or are simply easier to say.

Indeed a closer analysis of Freud's examples has undermined his original claims. In the case of the young man missing out the Latin word, it turns out that his 'wrong' version was more grammatically normal than the unusual language in which this particular verse was written. Theorising that the young man's mistake was due to an obscure chain of unconscious associations seems like an unnecessarily complex way to explain it.

Psychology professor James Reason proposes a simple criterion for deciding whether a slip is 'Freudian' (i.e. might have unconscious significance): 'For a slip to be convincingly Freudian, it should take a less familiar form than the intended word or action.' In other words, if you make a mistake that seems unlikely or difficult, such as mixing up your partner's name with that of an exotic foreign porn star specialising in bondage fetishism, it's probably no accident.

WANDERING THOUGHTS AND HANDS . . .

In his 1901 classic *The Psychopathology of Everyday Life*, Freud spelled out how such slips could reveal an unconscious thought, belief or wish. He explored in detail some specific examples. In one case a young man with whom he had shared a train journey had misquoted a line of Latin verse, missing out the word *aliquis* (someone). The young man asked Freud to help work out why he should have made such a mistake. A quick bout of word association led from *'aliquis'* to 'blood', whereupon the man revealed that he was worried about his girlfriend missing her period. Apparently his unconscious anxiety had acted to block the Latin word with the uncomfortable associations.

Another example Freud cited involved a doctor who was just concluding a housecall to a female patient when he realized that, even as he was saying goodbye, his hand was absent-mindedly tugging on the bow that held her nightgown closed. Freud reasoned that the doctor had repressed his feelings of lust for the patient, but these shameful desires were lurking in his unconscious, waiting to pounce as soon as his attention wandered. From such examples Freud concluded that most, if not all, such slips were unconsciously controlled.

GAGE

O N 13 SEPTEMBER 1848, Phineas Gage was working as the foreman of a railroad construction crew outside a town in Vermont when he was involved in one of the most celebrated industrial accidents of all time. Compacting gunpowder with a tool called a tamping bar, he made a spark that lit the powder, and the resulting explosion blew the tamping rod through his head. It entered his left cheek below the eye and exited at the top of his head, landing several feet away covered in blood and brain. Remarkably Gage survived and was conscious and talking within minutes, and thanks to the attentions of a local doctor, John Harlow, he was patched up and survived the subsequent infection. He died in 1860 after developing severe epilepsy.

Gage owes his place in the annals of psychology to an 1868 report Harlow compiled after his death, linking the precise location of his brain injury to peculiar changes in his personality and behaviour. Harlow claimed that before the injury Gage had been a solid, dependable fellow of even temperament and 'well-balanced mind', but said that after the accident 'the balance between his intellectual faculties and animal propensities seems to have been destroyed'. Apparently he was now foul-mouthed and self-indulgent, feckless, fitful and vacillating, unable to hold down his previous job or stick to any plans.

This was the first time that complex cognitive functions and personality traits had been localized in the brain, and Harlow's report was later seized upon as a clear demonstration that the frontal lobes controlled so-called executive capacities: foresight, planning, self-control and inhibition of 'animal instincts'. Psychologist and historian of the case Malcolm Macmillan comments that the status of the case 'is indexed by its still being cited in about two-thirds of all psychology and related neuroscience textbooks and by the fact that studies were still being undertaken some 150 years after the accident to establish which parts of Gage's brain were damaged'.

Macmillan has also discovered, however, a number of problems with the way Gage's case has been reported and used over the years, problems that tend to undermine its utility. The traditional account repeated in most textbooks has the post-accident Gage reduced to exhibiting himself as a curiosity at Barnum's circus before descending into drunkenness and even, in some versions, child-molesting. In fact, while there is evidence that Gage did briefly give public lectures, accompanied by his tamping rod, of which he had grown unaccountably fond, it is also known that he subsequently held down some demanding jobs including working as a stagecoach driver in Chile. There is no evidence that he became a drunk or sex pest, and no evidence beyond Harlow's sketchy claims for his personality before or after the accident. Modern reconstructions of the precise brain injury are based on Gage's skull, and disagree on the precise location.

It turns out that Gage's case is quite useless for drawing any precise conclusions about localization of brain function, but this hasn't stopped psychologists past and present from co-opting him as proof for their pet theories. As Macmillan comments, 'Phineas' story is worth remembering because it illustrates how easily a small stock of facts can be transformed into popular and scientific myth.'

GROUPTHINK

The tendency for groups of people to get important decisions badly wrong because they share illusions of infallibility and act to avoid, ignore or dismiss contradictory evidence.

W HY DO GROUPS OF PEOPLE responsible for big decisions sometimes get them so badly wrong, despite having information that should have prevented them from doing so? US psychologist Irving Lester Janis (1918–90) introduced the term 'groupthink' in 1971 to explain this apparent phenomenon, citing notorious historical mistakes such as the US failure to heed warnings that an attack on Pearl Harbor was imminent in 1941, or the ill-fated Bay of Pigs incident in which a poorly prepared attempt to invade Cuba ended in disaster in 1961.

Janis identified a number of mechanisms at work in groupthink. Group members reinforced each other in the belief they were morally superior and their decisions were infallible; they had stereotypical and unrealistic views of opponents; there was strong conformity pressure from within the group to prevent dissent from consensus, leading to the illusion of unanimity; information that contradicted the consensus was screened out, sometimes by group members acting as self-appointed protectors of the consensus. Groups thus became isolated from reality and fell victim to the Pygmalion effect, moulding interpretations of evidence to fit their preconceived notions and create self-fulfilling prophecies.

In this way, for instance, the US government in 1941 could discount clear evidence that Japanese forces were moving to strike at Pearl Harbour. A more recent example might be the way in which the Bush administration selectively ignored evidence that Saddam Hussein did not have weapons of mass destruction in the build-up to the Iraq War of 2003.

Janis' groupthink model quickly caught on and has proved enduringly popular. But the evidence underpinning the model is shaky and it has been accused of being restrictive and failing to adapt to the findings of subsequent research. Interestingly, related criticisms have been levelled at one of the model's main components: conformity pressure. In a landmark 1951 experiment, Polish-born US psychologist Solomon Elliott Asch (1907–96) showed that up to seventy-five per cent of people would knowingly give the wrong response to a simple question if everyone else in their group had previously given the incorrect response. This was interpreted as proof of the overwhelming power of the urge to conform. Critics later suggested that Asch's finding was 'a child of its time', and indeed when the experiment was repeated in 1980, a participant conformed with the incorrect majority just once out of 396 trials. The times, they had a'changed.

HALLUCINATION

Normally a perception is linked, albeit tenuously or indirectly, with sensory information from the outside world, known as external stimuli. A hallucination is a perception that has no accompanying external stimuli.

THE WORD ITSELF COMES from the Greek *aluô*, meaning 'to wander in mind' or 'to talk without reason'. Its use to describe a psychological phenomenon dates back to Jean-Etienne Esquirol (1772–1840), a French physician who pioneered the study of psychiatry. In the early 1800s he wrote: 'A person is said to labour under a hallucination, or to be a visionary, who has a thorough conviction of the perception of a sensation, when no external object, suited to excite this sensation, has impressed the senses.'

Esquirol contrasted hallucinations with illusions (see page 118), which are faulty perceptions of real external stimuli.

TRIP THE LIGHT FANTASTIC

Although hallucinations are today strongly associated with extremes of human experience – psychosis and mind-bending drug trips – they are surprisingly common and widespread, occurring in perfectly healthy, sane individuals. Up to 10 per cent of people experience hallucinations; considerably more if the definition is allowed to include sleep-related phenomena such as hypnogogic/hypnopompic hallucinations (experienced while drifting off to or awakening from sleep) or even dreams.

The range of conditions and triggers associated with hallucinations offer important clues to their origins and mechanism. For instance, hallucinations are sometimes experienced by people with epilepsy or migraine, often in the 'aura' phase that signals an imminent attack. In such cases the hallucination seems to be linked to bursts of activity in specific brain regions; for instance, uncontrolled firing of neurons in the temporal lobes, associated with both hearing and the sense of smell, may give rise to auditory or olfactory hallucinations. For one migraine sufferer, the smell of burnt rubber signals onset of an attack.

In these cases specific overexcitement of the cortex of the brain seems to trigger perceptions. In psychosis, hallucinations are often linked with general overexcitement or 'arousal' of the nervous system; there is so much mental 'noise' that it gives rise to hallucinatory perceptions. This mechanism for the generation of hallucination is backed up by evidence that hallucinations can be induced through sensory flooding and overload, such as in prisoners played loud music and subjected to other stressful stimuli.

However, absence or unusually low levels of stimuli are also linked to hallucination. For instance, people in sensory-deprivation experiments hallucinate, while a fascinating category of hallucination is linked to missing limbs and blindness. Amputees often report 'phantom limb' syndrome – the hallucination that the missing limb is present and is itchy or in pain. People whose eyesight or hearing has failed report visual or auditory hallucinations, almost as if the brain is 'compensating' with perceptions that 'ought' to be present. For instance, Charles Bonnet syndrome is the occurrence of visual hallucinations in mainly elderly people suffering from degenerative eye disease. Named for the eighteenth-century natural scientist who first described the syndrome in his own grandfather, it is characterized by unusual features such as people with strange hairstyles or headgear. In all these cases it seems as though understimulation of the normal perceptual channels causes the brain to substitute internally generated perceptions.

Elderly people suffering from Charles Bonnet syndrome often recognize that although their hallucinations look genuine they cannot be real; such perceptions are sometimes called pseudo-hallucinations. By contrast, psychotics may insist that their hallucinations are real even when it is proved that they cannot be. Some hallucinations seem so typical of psychosis that they are taken as diagnostic symptoms, for instance, 'hearing voices': auditory hallucinations that comment on the sufferer and his/her actions. Sometimes schizophrenics or manic depressives hear their own thoughts being spoken aloud, either as they think them (known as *Gedankenlautwerden*) or after a delay in *echo de la pensée* (thought echo).

Other sources of hallucination include sleep deprivation, hypnosis and trance states and drugs. Many of the classic hallucinogenic drugs, such as psilocybin, LCD, mescaline, cannabis and ergotamine seem to act by boosting nerve transmission and overloading perceptual processing systems with signal noise, apparently mimicking the mechanism at work in psychosis. Accordingly they are sometimes known as psychotomimetics.

HALO EFFECT

Also known as the atmosphere effect and the halo error, the halo effect is the tendency to allow favourable perception of one trait or thing to influence perception of other traits even though there may not be an actual link between them.

THE CLASSIC EXAMPLE is that someone perceived as handsome is attributed other favourable traits, such as intelligence, charm, competence, etc. The opposite of the halo effect is known as the horns effect or devil effect – the tendency to allow an unfavourable perception to colour perception of other aspects of a person or thing. This tendency is sometimes called the 'give a dog a bad name' effect.

The halo effect was first proposed by US psychologist Frederick Lyman Wells (1884–1964) in 1907 but didn't get its name or an actual demonstration that it existed until 1920, when US psychologist Edward Lee Thorndike (1874–1949) introduced the term 'halo error'. The effect is seen in fields as diverse as education, marketing, business and personality testing. Teachers, for instance, are likely to give a better grade for the same work to a student perceived as 'good' than one with a bad reputation. Consumers are likely to make purchasing decisions based on the halo effect generated by brands (e.g. a fan of Apple computers might buy a TV from the same company solely because of the reputation of the brand). Managers are advised to be careful of halo errors or horns errors when appraising staff; a common mistake, for instance, is to assume that someone with an engineering degree will be a competent manager, or that someone who likes to socialize will be a good sales person. In personality testing the halo effect undermines the reliability and validity of personality rating scales.

Intensive training can help to overcome the halo effect, but why does it exist in the first place? This and related perceptual biases are thought to reflect the heuristic nature of human reasoning, judgement and perception. Heuristic means 'rule of thumb' and refers to the cognitive short cuts used to save time in making decisions based on complex data, a vital skill for survival and success. Evolution favours the development of heuristic biases, but these in turn lead to phenomena such as the halo effect.

BLOWING HOT AND COLD

The halo effect is an example of a perceptual bias and a form of prejudice. It is linked to the phenomenon of trait centrality, discovered by Solomon Asch in 1946. Asch presented judges with a list of characteristics of a supposed individual – intelligent, skilful, industrious, warm, determined, practical and cautious – and asked them to evaluate further attributes of the target. By changing 'warm' to 'cold', Asch was able to elicit completely different attributions, so that 91 per cent of judges thought the 'warm' person would also be generous versus only 9 per cent for the 'cold' person. Warm/cold appears to be an example of a 'central trait', capable of generating halo/horns effect in subsequent judgements.

HYPNOSIS

*Hypnosis appears to be a special psychological
state with specific characteristics such as trance and
suggestibility. Modern definitions describe it as a
relationship between hypnotist and subject (who
may be the same person), which may or may not
represent an altered state of consciousness.*

SIMILAR OR RELATED PHENOMENA can be found in
all cultures and throughout history, usually in a
religious/mystical setting, but the modern concept
of hypnosis has its roots in mesmerism. In the
eighteenth century, Austrian doctor Franz Anton
Mesmer (1734–1815) claimed that a fluid force
called animal magnetism could be manipulated and
directed, producing remarkable psychological and
physical effects. A French Royal Commission, headed

by Benjamin Franklin, concluded that mesmerism was groundless and its effects due to imagination and suggestion, but interest in the phenomena uncovered by Mesmer continued. In the nineteenth century, Scottish doctor James Braid (1795–1860) proposed the term hypnosis, from the Greek for 'sleep state', and the practice played a major role in the development of psychiatry. Hypnosis was used by Charcot, Breuer and Freud, prompting the latter to develop his theories about the role of the unconscious. In 1933, American psychologist Clark Hull produced experimental backing for claims that hypnosis produced genuine and reproducible effects including anaesthesia, analgesia (pain relief) and amnesia. Subsequently hypnosis has been used in a wide variety of settings, from psychotherapy to law and order, and from entertainment to New Age and alien-abduction research. In almost all cases it remains controversial and misconceptions abound.

Freud quickly abandoned hypnosis (see page 92) on the basis that not everybody was susceptible to it, and since then scales to measure susceptibility to hypnosis show that about fifteen per cent of the population are resistant to hypnosis and about fifteen per cent are highly susceptible. Measures of susceptibility are consistent and stable, suggesting that it is a personality trait. Belief in the reality of hypnosis is the greatest predictor of hypnotic responsiveness.

But not everyone does believe that hypnosis is real, in the sense of being a genuine special state of consciousness. This goes against the popular image of hypnosis, which is marked out as unusual and even somehow occult because of the way in which experiences under hypnosis, in the words of J. F. Kihlstrom, 'are associated with a degree of subjective conviction bordering on delusion and an experienced involuntariness bordering on compulsion'. Yet the more closely such claims are investigated, the less convincing they become, and many researchers believe that hypnosis is not a special or different state of consciousness.

According to this 'non-state' account of hypnosis, the phenomenon can be explained by a sociocognitive hypothesis, which holds that hypnosis is a social construct and a learned behaviour, the product of tacit agreement by hypnotizer and hypnotized to follow an implicit script/role play, within a setting where such behaviour is both expected and permitted. This can be clearly seen in stage-show settings of hypnosis, but equally applies to hypnotherapy, where hypnosis is simply a form of placebo effect, sharing with it characteristics such as suggestion, a motivated client and a plausible system in a clinical setting. Many popular beliefs about hypnosis are myths, for instance, it does not improve memory/recall and in fact use of hypnosis to 'recover' memories is dangerous and harmful and results in false memories (see page 88). People cannot be hypnotized against their will, and hypnotic subjects are not turned into mindless automatons under the control of their hypnotists.

On the other hand, hypnotized people *can* apparently control normally involuntary, unconscious body processes, such as dilation of blood vessels to control blood flow. Such effects seem to suggest that maybe the 'state theory' of hypnosis is true, and that something truly special and remarkable is going on.

ILLUSION

Misperception of a stimulus, such as an image or sound, or the stimulus that generates the misperception.

ALTHOUGH THERE ARE SIMILARITIES, illusions are different from delusions and hallucinations (see pages 62 and 106 respectively). Illusions are entertaining but also valuable in psychology because of what they reveal about the process of perception.

Richard Gregory (1923–2010), one of the leading experts in the field, classified illusions into ambiguities, distortions, paradoxes and fictions. A simpler categorisation might be based on whether an illusion is created by properties of the environment; the physiology of the human perceptual system; the neuroanatomy of the brain; or the way the mind works (illusions of cognition). For instance, if you look at a pencil in a glass of water it seems crooked, because the water bends the light bouncing off the pencil. This illusion presumably pertains to any animal looking at the pencil, and also shows up on a photograph. This is an example of an optical illusion: one caused by the optical properties/characteristics of the stimulus. By contrast, the Müller-Lyer illusion (see page 35) doesn't even work on all humans, and seems to be the result of culturally ingrained rules of perspective. An illusion such as the disappearance of colours perceived when staring at a colourful pattern is caused by the biochemical properties of the pigment cells in the retina; the pigments that 'capture' and hence mediate perception of light of different colours get used up. The colours are still present, but cannot be registered by the eye.

Another way of classifying visual illusions is as geometrical illusions, illusions of lightness and illusions of representation. This last category has been likened to confusion of semantics versus confusion of syntax by analogy with language. Illusions of representation include ambiguous figures such as the well-known rabbit/duck and old crone/fashionable young lady pictures. Perception of ambiguous pictures 'flips'

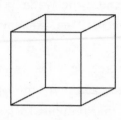

between interpretations. This is also seen in the Necker cube, which can be seen as receding or projecting from the viewer. This type of illusion is taken to show top-down processing at work. (The brain processes information from the eyes in two ways. Bottom-up processing starts with the cells in the retina, which detect brightness, edges and other simple features. Top-down processing is where the mind starts off with a pattern and fits the information to it.)

Television and cinema depend on the illusion of continuous motion; supplied with slightly differing successive static images, the brain 'fills in' the missing motion. Contrary to popular belief, this is not quite the same as persistence of vision, which is responsible for the illusions created by a thaumatrope ('turning

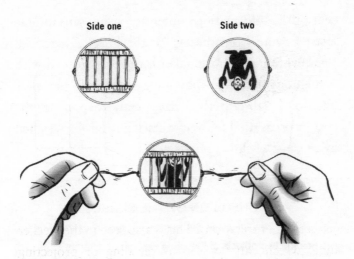

Side one   Side two

marvel'), a disc with a different picture on each side. If you spin it fast enough you see both pictures at the same time, because an image takes about 1/20 of a second to fade from your eye. Before the first image has faded you are already seeing the second one.

Why are we susceptible to illusions of cognition? Probably because perception is heuristic in nature – in order to speed up the translation of sensory data to conscious perception, our cognitive processes take short cuts and use generally applicable and broadly accurate rules of thumb to process the raw information and compensate for flaws in the incoming data stream. Gregory estimates, for instance, that up to ninety per cent of the information content of visual sensation is lost en route from the eye to the brain. There is a clear evolutionary rationale for this: confronted with ambiguous data that may indicate either a harmless bush or a sabre-toothed tiger ready to pounce, the cost of occasional faulty processing is far outweighed by the cost of slow processing.

CONFUSION OF THE SENSES

Illusions can affect all the senses. A simple example is holding two objects of the same weight but different sizes. The smaller object feels heavier, perhaps to compensate for the fact that it 'shouldn't' be as heavy as a bigger object. If one hand is immersed in cold water and the other in hot, and then both are placed in the same tub of water, each hand will give different sensations of warmth. If water is tasted after tasting salt, it seems sour, but after tasting sugar it seems bitter. Tap someone's arm at three spots 10 cm apart, in three bursts of five taps at each location, and they will report a series of fifteen successive pats running up their arm like a rabbit (this is known as the cutaneous rabbit illusion). By far the most studied illusions, however, are visual ones.

INVISIBLE GORILLA

The invisible gorilla is a person in a gorilla suit who appears halfway through a video in an experiment exploring a phenomenon called inattentional blindness.

IN THE EXPERIMENT PEOPLE are asked to watch a video of students passing a basketball and count the number of passes made by players wearing white. Amazingly around fifty per cent of people do not notice the gorilla who wanders through. Because the test subjects are focused on one particular aspect of the video, they are blind to the gorilla – it is effectively invisible.

The invisible gorilla first appeared in a 1999 study titled 'Gorillas in Our Midst' by Daniel Simons and Christopher Chabris. They were building on earlier studies where people failed to notice someone

opening an umbrella, although it turns out that something very similar to the invisible gorilla effect was inadvertently demonstrated by parapsychologist Tony Cornell as early as 1959. Cornell dressed up as a ghost and walked across the stage in a movie theatre during the trailers; polled later, thirty-two per cent of people claimed to have seen nothing. A more recent version of the invisible gorilla appeared in a 2009 study titled 'Did you see the unicycling clown?', which demonstrated inattentional blindness in people talking on a mobile phone.

MONKEY BUSINESS

Can it really be possible not to notice someone in a gorilla suit? Inattentionally blind people are not consciously aware of perceiving the gorilla, but it may be that they are perceiving it on an unconscious level – our senses take in far more information than makes it through to our conscious awareness (see, for instance, the cocktail party effect, page 42). Inattentional blindness has serious implications for tasks such as driving and piloting aircraft. Airline pilots focused intensely on their target runway might fail to perceive important objects like other aircraft.

In 2010 Simons and Chabris followed up their original study with a variant called 'Monkey Business'. The video presented seems the same; viewers are expecting to see the gorilla and they duly do so. However, very few of them notice the two other striking features of the video – the curtain at the back changes colour and one of the players wanders off. Expecting the unexpected doesn't help you to spot it.

LAING AND ANTI-PSYCHIATRY

Ronald David Laing (1927–1989) was a Scottish psychiatrist, social critic, author and philosopher, who at one time was the most widely read psychiatrist in the world. He was the father of anti-psychiatry, a movement that challenged traditional views of mental illness and its treatment, with great resonance for wider society, particularly in the late 1960s and early 1970s.

After training at the Tavistock Clinic in London, a renowned centre of psychoanalysis, Laing, with others, developed the precepts of anti-psychiatry, arguing for madness as a social construct – the result of social pressures. Schizophrenia, for instance, was explained as a rational response to irrational circumstances, especially contradictory communication patterns in families – a classic example being the statement, 'You don't love me, you only pretend that you do,' which simultaneously demands and precludes a declaration of love – an account which seems to blame some of the victims of mental illness for its genesis. According to anti-psychiatry, schizophrenic experience has value: it can be cathartic and transformative.

In anti-psychiatry, psychosis is seen as a shamanistic journey – a way to express the oppressive effects of socialization – while psychiatry is seen as dehumanizing and oppressive, with disastrous twin consequences of both psychiatric oppression and psychiatric dependence, whereby people fail to face up to and deal with life's problems. Ironically such aspects of anti-psychiatry, a quintessentially counter-cultural movement, closely resemble reactionary critiques of psychotherapy. Anti-psychiatry was not the only attack on psychiatry originating at this time. Hungarian-American psychoanalyst and moral philosopher Thomas Szasz (1920–2012), though a bitter opponent of anti-psychiatry, struck at the moral, legal and philosophical legitimacy of psychiatry, arguing that mental illness was an illegitimate extension of biological models into psychology.

The label anti-psychiatry was actually coined by psychiatrist David Cooper, who collaborated with

Laing on the Kingsley Hall project in East London, an ambitious and idealistic attempt to create a non-hierarchical community in which therapists would live side by side with the mentally ill. Running from 1965 to 1970, Kingsley Hall was highly controversial, and widely perceived to have been discredited by the 1971 publication of *Mary Barnes: Two Accounts of A Journey Through Madness*, written by one of the patients there, Mary Barnes, and her psychiatrist, Joseph Berke.

It was during this period that Laing wrote probably his most influential book, *The Politics of Experience and the Bird of Paradise* (1967), a critique of Western society which argued that psychologically restrictive values caused widespread unhappiness. Anticipating the student protests of May 1968, the book was very much in tune with the sentiments of the time. The first part, *The Politics of Experience*, is characterized by what lecturer in Cultural Studies Mark Patterson calls 'pseudo-gnomic utterances' (for example, 'We require a history of phenomena, not simply more phenomena of history'), while the *Bird of Paradise* is a prose-poem, described by Patterson as 'horrific and amusing, often portentous and indulgent.'

The anti-psychiatry movement is generally seen to have failed by mental health professionals because its therapeutic techniques don't relieve the distressing experiences of schizophrenia. Yet communities similar to Kingsley Hall flourished for decades under the auspices of Laing's umbrella organisation, the Philadelphia Association. While anti-psychiatry is today seen as a product of its time, its legacy has profoundly and irreversibly changed attitudes to mental illnesses and their treatment.

LITTLE ALBERT

L ITTLE ALBERT WAS THE SUBJECT of one of the most famous and controversial experiments in psychology, carried out by John B. Watson (1878–1958), progenitor of the behaviourist movement. In a 1920 paper, Watson and his graduate student Rosalie Raynor described a classical conditioning experiment on an infant they called Albert B, although he has become known as 'Little Albert' and it has since been discovered that his real name was Douglas Merritte. Watson argued that infants are *tabula rasae*, 'blank tablets', and that all personality and behaviour are conditioned by environmental influences. In the last experiment of his career, he set out to provide experimental backing for some of his basic claims by carrying out a form of Pavlovian conditioning with a human rather than canine subject.

Little Albert was nine months old when the experiments began at Johns Hopkins paediatric hospital. Watson wrote that the infant had been selected because he was healthy and seemed temperamentally robust. Initially he was presented with a range of stimuli – unconditioned stimuli (UCS) in the lexicon of behaviourism – including a white rat, a rabbit and even a burning newspaper. Little Albert displayed no fear in response to any of them. He did, however, get frightened and start crying when a steel bar was struck with a claw hammer behind his back.

Two months later Little Albert was again shown the white rat, but this time the presentation was accompanied by a frightening strike of the hammer on the steel bar whenever he touched the rat. After seven pairings of the rat and noise (in two sessions, one week apart), Albert reacted by crying and attempting to flee (he had to be caught before he fell off the table) when the rat was presented without the loud noise. Albert had been conditioned to fear the rat. What's more, testing with a variety of other white, furry things including a rabbit, a bearded Santa Claus mask and Watson's own hair showed that this conditioned reflex had been generalized to other stimuli. A month later Albert's mother moved and Watson claimed it was not possible to follow up with the infant.

Even at the time there were questions about whether the Little Albert experiment was ethical. Watson defended himself by arguing that the ends justified the means: 'They [such experiments] will be worth all they cost if through them we can find a method which will help us remove fear.' Little Albert became a fixture of psychology textbooks and entered psychology folklore, with humorous speculation as to whether he grew up with an irrational phobia of white furry things.

In 2009, however, after a seven-year search, psychologist Hall P. Beck revealed the true, sad tale of Little Albert, identifying him as Douglas Merritte, son of a wet nurse at the hospital where the experiments had been carried out. He had died of hydrocephalus at the age of six, and further research by Alan J. Fridlund and others revealed that he had suffered from the condition since birth. Watson must have known at the very least that the boy suffered cognitive impairment, in direct opposition to his claims in the 1920 paper. Fridlund has said that he's arrived at the 'nearly inescapable conclusion that [Watson] knew of Albert's condition and intentionally misrepresented it'. It is possible that Watson chose Douglas because his cognitive impairment made him relatively unresponsive to stimuli such as animals, at least at first; a 'normal' baby might have been scared from the start, contradicting Watson's claim that all children are born without fear of animals, and only acquire it through conditioning. It also seems likely that Douglas was chosen because his mother worked for the hospital and hence felt pressured to consent to what would clearly be a distressing procedure for her child.

Beck and Fridlund point out that Watson built much of his subsequent career on the back of the Little Albert experiment: 'Advertising himself as an expert on child development, Watson developed the cover story that Douglas/Albert was "healthy" and "normal," and used the "Little Albert" study as one of the bases for the best-selling *Psychological Care of the Infant and Child* (1928), which preached regimentation and stoicism over spontaneity and nurturance, and profoundly influenced the ways of child rearing for generations to come.' But since Little Albert was not a healthy child, whatever value the study may have had is destroyed, along with the remains of Watson's reputation.

MASLOW AND HIS HIERARCHY OF NEEDS

ABRAHAM MASLOW (1908–1970) was an American psychologist influential in what was known as Third Force psychology, a movement that attempted to forge a more humanistic approach to personal psychology, and which inaugurated a reorientation of psychology towards happiness and well-being. Today, optimal psychology (the psychology of optimising personal achievement, professional performance and psychological well-being) is all the rage; much of it can be traced back to the theories of Maslow. He in turn was influenced by existentialism, the Jungian concept of individuation and dissatisfaction with prevailing behaviourist and psychoanalytic schools of psychology (Maslow had begun his career as a behaviourist).

His major contribution is his hierarchy of needs, a theory about the needs that govern human behaviour, generating personal values and the cognitions and behaviour that spring from them. According to Maslow, people have lower or basic 'deficiency' needs and higher or meta- 'growth' needs. The basic needs include hunger, thirst and shelter; safety; belonging and being loved; and self-esteem. Meta-needs are subsumed under the heading 'self-actualization', a term originally introduced by Kurt Goldstein (1878–1965), to describe what he saw as the sole true motive of human psychology, and which built on Jung's individuation concept.

To self-actualize successfully, a person must meet needs as diverse as justice, wholeness, beauty, individuality and autonomy; self-actualization requires qualities such as a philosophical sense of humour, a tendency to form few but deep friendships, resistance to external pressure and transcendence of the environment rather than simply coping. Maslow also recognized higher needs beyond self-actualization, such as discovery, transcendence and aesthetics. Meeting these needs could lead to peak experiences: moments of transcendence that could take a person beyond self-actualization to what Maslow called the Z realm, a realm that transcends space and time, characterized by profound feelings of spontaneity and harmony with the universe. Peak experience is sometimes also known as oceanic feeling.

There are some problems with Maslow's scheme. A movement known as socioanalytic theory highlights incompatibility between the needs of belonging and self-esteem, 'getting along' and 'getting ahead' – the former stresses compliance and conformity, the latter involves rejecting these, creating a constant social tension even for well-adjusted, effective people as they seek to balance meeting the needs for belonging and self-esteem.

Maslow appears not to have spotted this incompatibility, but he did recognize the difficulty of self-actualization: his 1970 list of examples included only nine historical (including Beethoven, Einstein, Lincoln, Jefferson, Thoreau, Eleanor Roosevelt and Walt Whitman) and nine living people. Building on the Maslow approach, clinical psychologist Dr Ted Landsman described such an optimally functioning type as 'the Beautiful and Noble Person' (this was in the 1970s).

Maslow rejected the mechanistic approach of science as inappropriate for psychology, stressing a holistic, humanistic approach. His theory, with its humane and positive messages, has had wide appeal.

It is particularly popular with students, according to the *Biographical Dictionary of Psychology*, 'partly because it is simple and plausible, and partly because they are likely to have seen it before [in a range of textbooks]'. Critics contend that his theories are simply secular ideologies substituting for religion, confusing theory with ideology and rhetoric with research, and are untestable and hence unfalsifiable.

MILGRAM AND THE OBEDIENCE TO AUTHORITY EXPERIMENTS

A SERIES OF FAMOUS EXPERIMENTS carried out by Stanley Milgram in New Haven, Connecticut in the early 1960s seemed to show that perfectly ordinary people would inflict painful and possibly lethal electric shocks simply because they were told to.

Milgram's research caused a sensation, and was widely interpreted in the light of the Nazi death camps and the disturbing psychology of the Holocaust. But had Milgram really uncovered dark truths about humanity and the power of authority to pervert individual conscience? Or had he conducted a deeply unethical experiment that ranks among the most misinterpreted studies of all time?

Stanley Milgram was a social psychologist, motivated in part by the difficult questions thrown up by the Holocaust. What kind of people had staffed the death camps, and how could so many have committed such appalling atrocities? Between 1960 and 1963, while teaching at Yale, he conducted a series of variations on an experimental set-up in which people were recruited at random from the phone book and asked to help with what they believed was a study aimed at improving education techniques.

The recruits were shown a dashboard that apparently controlled an electric-shock apparatus, which was demonstrated by giving them a mild but painful shock, supposedly of forty-five volts. Then they were introduced to a test 'subject' (actually one of the research team) who was strapped into an electric chair. During the test the recruits could not see the 'subject' but they could hear him. A 'supervisor' stood by to prompt the recruit, and he was told to administer increasingly large shocks each time the 'subject' got a question wrong. The controls had a dial with the voltages marked on it, together with warnings such as 'Danger – severe shock'. As the test progressed the 'subject' began to cry out and object, even claiming to have a heart condition. If the recruits objected or hesitated, the 'supervisor' pressured them to continue.

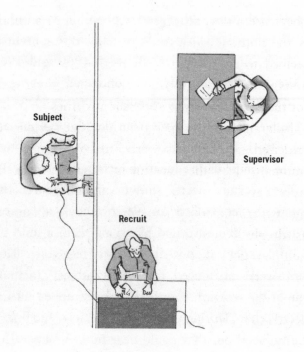

Milgram found that around two-thirds of recruits would administer what they believed to be real electric shocks, all the way up to the highest setting of 400 volts, even after the 'subject' had screamed and then gone quiet. This amazing finding was interpreted as proof that for the majority of people the urge to obey an authority figure was more powerful than morality or empathy. Here then was the key to the horrors of the Holocaust – human beings are creatures of obedience and conformity, and bowing to authority is the natural order. In particular, the experiment seemed to show that when recruits started off by administering mild shocks, it was then much easier for them to progress to apparent atrocities.

Milgram and his experiment have been extensively criticized. The recruits were often upset and even traumatized by the experiment, during which they were remorselessly pressured and even bullied by the experimenters. Today this set-up is regarded as deeply flawed and unethical. The widespread interpretation of the experiment, still current today in popular discussion, has also been critiqued. The 'supervisors' continually insisted that the 'shocks' being administered were not dangerous, and the Milgram experiments are now believed to say more about the way in which trust is the default mode for interactions between people. The recruits trusted the 'supervisors' when they said the shocks were safe and that it was necessary for the experiment to continue.

Claims that the Milgram studies tell us much about the Holocaust also fall short; the perpetrators in the death camps were well aware that they were doing real harm and they were not acting in the face of moral doubt or revulsion. Despite the moral panic that followed Milgram's findings, he had emphatically *not* proved that the good people of New Haven, Connecticut, were just a step away from becoming concentration-camp guards.

PAVLOV'S DOG

An animal used in experiments by the Russian physiologist Ivan Pavlov (1849–1936), but the term has since come to mean anything (including a person) that responds reflexively and unthinkingly to a stimulus of some sort. In the original experiments such stimuli included anything from shapes and colours to musical tones and, most famously, the ringing of a bell.

B Y THE TIME HE CAME to perform the studies for which he is best remembered today, Pavlov was already a celebrated physiologist whose research into nervous control of the digestive system had put him on track to win the Nobel prize, which he duly did in 1904. Early in his career he joined the Heidenhain laboratory in Breslau, where dogs were being used to study the circulatory system. His brilliant surgical technique enabled him to create 'living windows' into the physiology of the dog without killing it. He could draw part of the stomach through the abdominal wall to create external pouches for direct study and sampling, and later he perfected the technique of making slits in the throat so that food could be intercepted before it reached the stomach. Pavlov emphasized the need to study physiology in the context of the whole, living animal, creating an apparatus by which saliva and gastric juices could be collected independently and measured, offering a way to quantify physiological and nervous responses. The Pavlov dog had become an experimental technology in itself, one that Pavlov would eventually use to probe the innermost processes of the brain.

In the course of his work Pavlov observed that the dogs began salivating on sight of lab workers, evidently anticipating the delivery of food; he called this 'psychic salivation'. Well versed in Darwin's theories on animal behaviour and the adaptive role of instinct, and also in the work of I. M. Sechenov, who argued that all mental events were reflexes, Pavlov decided to investigate psychic salivation.

In a series of classic experiments he showed that it

was possible to train a dog to associate the prospect of food with a stimulus unconnected to food (a neutral stimulus), so that the dog responded to the neutral stimulus by salivating copiously in the same way as it would respond to a more logical stimulus such as the presentation of a bowl of food. Pavlov called this new response the conditional response (CR), while the original response was the unconditional response (UCR). Normally the UCR is elicited by an unconditional stimulus (UCS), but through the process of conditioning, a neutral stimulus (NS) becomes a conditional stimulus (CS), which elicits a CR. In translation 'conditional' became 'conditioned', so that in the English-speaking world CS and CR stand for conditioned stimulus and reflex. The French still use Pavlov's original version. The process as a whole is now known as classical conditioning, and thanks to Pavlov's jargon it became possible to describe a process that was at least partly psychological in almost algebraic fashion:

$$UCS \rightarrow UCR$$
$$NS + UCS \rightarrow UCR$$
$$NS = CS$$
$$CS \rightarrow CR$$

1. *Before conditioning: UCS and CS are not associated*

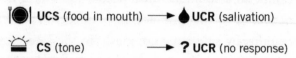

2. *During conditioning: dog begins to make associations*

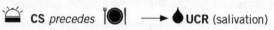

3. *After conditioning: bell and salivation are associated*

Pavlov interpreted classical conditioning in Darwinian terms, as a process that allows animals to develop temporary reflexes, with great adaptive value in a changing and unpredictable environment. The phenomenon became the basis for a truly scientific psychology, in both theory and practice, with enormous impact on the rising school of psychology known as behaviourism (see Skinner Box, page 177). Not only did classical conditioning offer a model for understanding animal, and by extension human behaviour, but once conditioning had been established, the CR salivation could further be used as an objective, quantitative way to measure aspects of canine perception. For instance, could dogs keep track of time or distinguish between colours, range of tones or differences between shapes? Pavlov's dogs offered scientific psychology the experimental paradigm of its dreams, one with the potential to change completely the status of psychology.

Pavlov and his team started to explore psychological dimensions of conditioning after accidentally making a dog neurotic. An unfortunate test subject was conditioned to respond to a circle as the CS, and also to associate an ellipse with not being fed. The dog was then presented with ellipses that became progressively more rounded, until it was difficult to distinguish between ellipse and circle. Although the dog seemed able to make the fine judgement, the uncertainty apparently took a psychic toll and the poor animal became distressed and agitated. Pavlov called this experimental neurosis. His interest in the interplay between the innate systems of nervous control and the way that behaviour could be modified led him to set up an institute for research into the genetics of behaviour shortly before his death in 1936, by which time he was the Grand Old Man of Soviet science and a cultural icon.

PENIS ENVY

A concept from Freudian psychoanalysis, describing the emotion experienced by young girls aged 3–6 on discovering that boys have penises but they do not.

FREUD DEVELOPED THIS CONCEPT as part of his theory about the stages of psychosexual development and the psychic crises he called the Oedipal conflict and castration anxiety. According to Freud's account, the phallic or Oedipal stage of childhood, around ages 3–6, is characterized by the discovery of the genitals. By genitals Freud meant penis, since in his system the penis was the superior and effectively the only organ; he based this claim on the observation that when a child sees another naked child, there is either a visible sexual organ, i.e. a penis, or no visible sexual organ. Freud explained that a boy seeing a naked girl for the first time would realize that some people do not have penises, and would conclude that he might lose his, triggering overwhelming castration anxiety. This anxiety and the related Oedipal anxieties felt by the boy are so profound that sexual urges are driven into the unconscious (known as latency) while at the same time the moral supervisor of the superego is created.

Turning to the female, Freud explained that a little girl's response to the revelation of the penis is to assume that she has already been castrated, and to blame this on the mother, who has also suffered this dreadful fate. The penis is perceived as superior and the girl feels inherently inferior. She develops a profound longing for a penis of her own, hence penis envy, and this desire is so great it causes her to reject the mother and become oriented to her father, and by extension men in general, as the ones who can give her a penis substitute in the form of a child. As with boys, latency and the creation of the superego result from the feminine castration complex.

Penis envy and its male counterpart – castration anxiety – are thus the driving forces of psychic development and the root of personality, according to Freud's model. He considered the discovery of this epic psychic event his greatest achievement. For men and women alike, he wrote, 'anatomy is destiny'.

Not surprisingly Freud's whole narrative has been slammed as desperately misogynistic. Working from just a handful of cases, he concluded that penis envy led to development of a weaker superego and hence weaker moral sense in women, who were essentially incomplete males and hence inferior. Several female psychoanalysts rejected the penis-envy concept; Karen Horney, for instance, proposed that men actually suffer from womb envy. She was probably being at least partly satirical, but Freud failed to get the joke and his response revealed the fundamentally pseudoscientific nature of psychoanalysis by offering a clear example of unfalsifiability: 'We shall not be very greatly surprised if a woman analyst who has not been sufficiently convinced of the intensity of her own wish for a penis also fails to attach proper importance to that factor in her patients.' In other words, Horney's concept of womb envy must be the result of her penis envy; criticism becomes proof. In the end, however, Freud himself admitted that women remained a closed book to him. 'That is all I have to say to you about femininity,' he wrote in 1933. 'It is certainly incomplete and fragmentary and does not always sound friendly . . .'

PHALLIC SYMBOL

A symbolic representation of the penis. In fact, the word phallus on its own suffices in psychoanalytic discourse, because it is taken to indicate a symbolic penis rather than a real one.

FREUDIAN PSYCHOANALYSIS HAS BEEN character-ized as phallocentric, which seems accurate given the central role of the penis in the Oedipal and castration complexes, said to emerge during the phallic stage of psychosexual development. In a sense, concern and obsession with the penis lies at the heart of Freud's entire theory of personality and the psyche: he believed that the male psyche becomes defined by the fear of losing the penis and the female psyche by the desire to 'regain' one (see Penis Envy, page 148).

In Freud's day the penis was taboo; it was dangerous and transgressive for the concept to arise in the psyche, let alone in public discussion. Accordingly, the concept of this organ, so central to the architecture of the psyche, is repressed yet constantly seeks to emerge from the unconscious, and Freud believed that this is where symbolism comes into play. The way in which the conscious mind receives and deals with upwelling of repressed material from the unconscious is to dress it up in symbolism, and no symbol was more common or more important than the phallus. This held true even for women, because, Freud claimed, the penis is 'the more striking and for both sexes the more interesting component of the genitals'.

In his discussion of dream symbolism, Freud gave a list of phallic symbols that is exhaustive to the point of comedy. It ranged from the most basic and obvious symbols associated with the phallus by virtue of shape – sticks, umbrellas, posts, trees – to those linked by penetrative function – knives, daggers and spears. Firearms belonged to both these sets. The list included objects from which fluid could flow – taps, fountains, watering-cans – and what Freud described as 'objects which are capable of being lengthened', such as hanging lamps and extensible pencils. It even extended to 'balloons, flying machines and most recently Zeppelin airships' because all shared the 'remarkable characteristic of the male organ . . . to rise up in defiance of the laws of gravity'. Flying in a dream is also phallic: in flight, the phallus becomes 'the essence of the dreamer's whole person'; the dreamer as a giant, flying erection. Freud believed this is true of women too, because he saw the female clitoris as a mini-penis or at least penis-substitute:

> Remember that our dreams aim at being the fulfilments of wishes and that the wish to be a man is found so frequently, consciously or unconsciously, in women. Nor will anyone with a knowledge of anatomy be bewildered by the fact that it is possible for women to realize this wish through the same sensations as men. Women possess as part of their genitals a small organ similar to the male one; and this small organ, the clitoris, actually plays the same part in childhood and during the years before sexual intercourse as the large organ in men.

Freud's cataloguing of phallic symbols continued, encompassing clothing such as overcoats, hats, cloaks and neckties ('which hang down and are not worn by women'), and animals including reptiles, fish 'and above all the famous symbol of the snake'. Woods and bushes signalled pubic hair. He even recruited technology to his cause: 'the imposing mechanism of the male sexual apparatus explains why all kinds of complicated machinery which is hard to describe serve as symbols for it'.

Given such a catalogue, it is hardly surprising that the phallic symbol has become something of an Achilles heel for psychoanalysis, the source of much amusement and attacks on its credibility. Even when this problem was identified analysts did not resile from their enthusiasm for phallic symbolism; the Hungarian psychoanalyst Sandor Ferenczi deadpanned, 'The derisive remark was once made against psychoanalysis that the unconscious sees a penis in every convex object and a vagina or anus in every concave one. I find this sentence well characterizes the facts.'

SOMETIMES A CIGAR IS JUST A CIGAR

Perhaps the most famous phallic symbol associated with Freud is his cigar. He smoked twenty a day and considered them invaluable to his work and day-to-day existence, fiercely resisting attempts by doctors to convince him to quit despite the toll on his health. He would eventually develop fatal cancer of the mouth. Inevitably, Freud's cigars were identified as phallic symbols and made the butt of jokes, supposedly prompting the famous quote attributed to him: 'Sometimes a cigar is just a cigar.'

In fact, there is no evidence that he ever said this, and the quote first appears in the 1950s, long after his death. Quite to the contrary, it seems likely that contemporary psychoanalysis definitely did see the cigar as a phallus. In 1922 an article by Eric Hiller in *The International Journal of Psycho-Analysis* looked at the symbolism of smoking:

> Cigarettes and cigars can symbolize the penis. They are cylindrical and tubular. They have a hot, red end. They emit smoke that is fragant (= flatus = semen) . . . I refer to the reason, or at least one of the reasons, why people start smoking (and, of course, why they go on), that is the phallic significance of the cigarette, cigar and pipe. It is thus a substitute for the penis (mother's breast) of which they have been deprived (castrated, weaned).

Freud himself tentatively explored the psychology of his addiction to cigars. In letters to colleagues he suggested addiction to smoking might be a substitute to compensate for 'withdrawal symptoms' from addictive masturbation in childhood, even hinting that this might account for his own habit.

PHOBIAS

*A phobia is an extreme, irrational fear of a thing,
place or situation, far beyond anything that is
reasonable.*

SOMETIMES PHOBIAS WILL RELATE to things that seem
genuinely scary, such as snakes or being eaten, but
the point about a phobia is that it causes anxiety even
when there is little or no actual danger. For instance,
most people know when looking at a picture of a
snake that the picture itself cannot harm them, but
someone with a phobia of snakes may become very
upset.

According to the National Phobics Society, the eight
most common phobias in the UK (in descending order)
are: arachnophobia (fear of spiders), social phobia
(fear of meeting people or being at social events),

aeronausiphobia (fear of air sickness), agoraphobia (fear of crowds, public places and being away from a safe place), carcinophobia (fear of cancer), brontophobia (fear of thunder), thanatophobia (fear of death), and cardiophobia (fear of the heart and heart conditions). Interestingly, claustrophobia, the irrational fear of confined spaces, does not even make this list, despite being experienced by 1 in 10 people at some point in their lives, which goes to show how common some of these other phobias must be. For instance, 1 out of every 100 people suffers severe agoraphobia and 1 out of 8 may experience a mild version.

INCY WINCY SPIDER

Arachnophobia may be the most common phobia in the West, but in other parts of the world, including many areas where poisonous spiders are relatively common, this phobia is less often encountered. Why should arachnophobia be so culturally specific? One suggestion is that it is linked to historical beliefs about spiders dating back to medieval Europe, where there was a common (but misguided) belief that spiders could spread plague.

There is also evidence that some phobias or aspects of phobia may be hard-wired. For instance, another common phobia that doesn't feature in the top eight is acrophobia, fear of high places. This is commonly confused with vertigo, a form of dizziness and loss of balance, which is often a symptom of acrophobia and other phobias. A famous experiment with young children, known as the 'visual cliff', shows how the urge to avoid steep drops is built into us. Babies who have just learned to crawl are put on a table with a glass top, which gives the illusion of having a cliff-edge, and will typically refuse to crawl over the edge of the 'cliff' – they know to avoid it without ever having been taught. Perhaps humans have evolved to have a natural fear of such situations. A hi-tech form of the visual cliff, known as a 'virtual cliff', can even be used to treat acrophobia – experiments have shown that using virtual-reality goggles to simulate the experience of being near a cliff edge can help sufferers get over their fear of high places.

Some phobias can be fatal. Trypanophobia, fear of injections, is an extremely common phobia that affects at least one in ten people and causes a sudden collapse in blood pressure leading to fainting. At least twenty-three people have died as a result of this reaction.

PLACEBO EFFECT

A placebo is a treatment or that part of a treatment that has no 'active' content and should not be expected to produce an effect.

THE PLACEBO EFFECT is the improvement in outcome – i.e. improvement in health – due to the placebo treatment. The term comes from the Latin for 'to please', possibly via its use in the first line of the vespers for the dead, 'Placebo Domino . . .', sung by professional mourners at funerals in the Middle Ages. Placebo treatments can take many forms but the classic example is a sugar pill or saline solution that the patient believes contains medicine. Placebo effects have been claimed for almost all diseases and conditions, from pain to heart disease to warts to depression.

One of the earliest descriptions of the placebo effect in action comes from the sixteenth-century French essayist Michel de Montaigne. Writing in 1572 he related the story of:

> . . . a man who was sickly and subject to [kidney] stone who often resorted to enemas, which he had made up for him by physicians, and none of the usual formalities were omitted . . . Imagine him then, lying on his stomach, with all the motions gone through except that no application has been made! This ceremonial over, the apothecary would retire, and the patient would be treated just as if he had taken the enema; the effect was the same as if he actually had . . . When, to save the expense, the patient's wife tried sometimes to make do with warm water, the result betrayed the fraud; this method was found useless and they had to return to the first.

Montaigne's report even indicates a sort of controlled experiment, with the effect of the placebo compared to that of no placebo, apparently confirming the reality of the phenomenon. Nonetheless, doubts remain over the existence and strength of the placebo effect (see below).

Modern interest in the placebo effect strengthened after a 1955 study by H.K. Beecher which has been interpreted to show a placebo was fifty-six per cent as effective as morphine in post-operative pain relief. Since then, studies have shown that between thirty to forty per cent of patients show improvement following the administration of a placebo, across a wide range of mental and physical symptoms and disorders. With no side effects, no danger of overdose and no or minimal costs, placebos have something of the air of a wonder drug. Robert Buckman, oncologist, writer and broadcaster called them: 'the most adaptable, protean, effective, safe and cheap drugs in the world's pharmacopoeia'.

All of which raises an intriguing paradox. The ethics of medicine would seem to argue that the most efficacious treatment with the fewest side effects and the lowest cost should be the first one provided, yet ethical considerations militate against knowingly administering sham treatments as if they were genuine, and preclude charging for treatment known to be fake. It can only be ethical to treat with placebo if the treatment is given for free, but this will prevent it from working.

The placebo effect raises several questions. Is it real? How does it work? Why does it work? Some research challenges the existence and extent of the placebo effect, and there are several factors that can give rise to a fake placebo effect. For instance, disease is said to have a natural history, which means that over the course of a disease people feel worse at some times and better at others, and may eventually get better. Another confounding factor is reporting bias, for instance, patients may report feeling better after a treatment because of an unconscious desire to tell the experimenter what he wants to hear. The Hawthorne effect is a phenomenon where people change their behaviour because they are being observed. It was originally reported in workers, who were found to be more productive when being watched, but also applies to reports of pain relief because it has been found that male subjects in particular will tolerate higher levels of pain when being watched by an experimenter.

But there is also a great deal of evidence that the placebo effect is real, including studies showing physiological changes that would be hard to attribute to natural history or reporting bias. In one study researchers successfully treated people's warts by painting them with placebo and promising that by the time the colour wore off the wart would be gone. Other studies have shown that analgesic (pain relieving) placebo effect can be blocked by administering a drug called naxolone.

Given that the placebo effect is real, how might it work? One crucial element is the placebo message – the manner in which the patient picks up the message that a treatment will be effective. This message can be mediated in many ways, including learned associations, explicit instruction, rational argument, magical reasoning, trust in authority and bedside manner (shown to be especially important).

The effects of naxolone suggest a possible mechanism of action for analgesic placebo. Naxolone blocks receptors for endogenous opiates, aka endorphins – neurotransmitters produced by the body that are similar to and act in similar ways to opiates such as morphine – suggesting that the placebo effect is boosting production of these endorphins. Endorphins are involved in many aspects of the immune response such as inflammation, wound repair, blood flow, etc, so this could be the mechanism for most or all observed placebo effects.

Explaining why the placebo effect works is harder. One suggested evolutionary rationale for the placebo effect is that we have evolved to pick up and assess external prognostic cues (i.e. clues as to whether and how quickly we will get better), and use these to govern the commitment of resources to the healing process. Boosting the immune response to recover faster costs physiological resources, and if the prognosis for an individual is poor it may be better to husband resources for the long term by recovering more slowly or letting a disease takes its natural course. On the other hand, cues such as those involved in the placebo message ('I am a skilled healer', 'this is powerful medicine', 'hospitals make you better', etc.) signal a good prognosis, and the mind in turn mobilizes its resources for a speedy recovery – hence the placebo effect.

Other questions about the placebo effect remain. Why are there cross-cultural differences in the effect? For instance, placebo treatments achieve a sixty per cent healing rate for stomach ulcers in Germany, but just seven per cent in Brazil, while for the treatment of hypertension, placebo medicine is less effective in Germany than elsewhere.

THE NOCEBO EFFECT

The other side of the coin for the placebo effect is the nocebo effect, which is where stimuli that should be neutral have a detrimental effect, for example, someone who believes that a harmless sugar pill is poisonous may react accordingly. Extreme forms of the nocebo effect can be seen in the voodoo and Baskerville effects. The voodoo effect is where belief in the power of a voodoo curse produces extreme physical and mental consequences, such as believing and acting as if one has been turned into a zombie. The Baskerville effect is where superstitious belief or magical thinking causes death. It was first noted in a study that found that in Chinese and Japanese communities, where the number four has ominous superstitious associations, there was up to twenty-seven per cent increase in the chance of cardiac death on the fourth day of each month. The effect is named for the death of the fictional Sir Charles Baskerville, frightened to death by a spectral hound in the famous Sherlock Holmes story.

REICH

PSYCHOANALYST AND PSEUDOSCIENTIST, famous for his controversial theories on the power of the orgasm and the existence of orgasm energy, aka orgone, Wilhelm Reich (1897–1957) was a fascinating and divisive character. Born in part of the Austro-Hungarian Empire that is now Ukraine, his childhood, by his own account, was a torrid mix of sex and death. He claims to have been amazingly precocious, learning about sex at age four and losing his virginity at age eleven, but it was the events of his twelfth year that probably shaped his character. His oppressed mother started an affair with one of his tutors, and after spying on them he betrayed her to his father. Terrible scenes ensued, culminating in his mother committing suicide by the horrible and drawn-out method of drinking kitchen cleaner. After this Reich became obsessed with sex, visiting brothels and claiming to have had sex every day.

While training as a doctor in Vienna, Reich met Sigmund Freud, instantly falling under his spell and becoming heavily involved in psychoanalysis. He was particularly attracted by Freud's theories about sexuality and the importance of the libido, or sex drive, for personality and psychological health. Soon he was going far beyond the teachings of his mentor, championing progressive ideas about sexuality, particularly for young women, advocating contraception, family planning, abortion and active adolescent sexuality. He also slept with some of his patients and even married one.

Reich's transgressive views about sex alienated the Freudians, especially after the publication of his 1927 book *The Function of the Orgasm* in which he developed a philosophy of sexual energy as the core of human psychology. His experiences in counselling convinced him that sexual or orgasmic energy was a real physical force, and he became intent on proving it.

Meanwhile the antagonism of the Freudians had driven him to Germany, where he developed the sociological aspects of his philosophy, attempting to transform psychoanalysis into a movement for the people. He became a socialist firebrand and even visited Communist Russia in 1929. His brush with Communism would come back to haunt him in 1950s America, even though at the time he clear-sightedly exposed Stalinism as little more than dressed-up fascism. In 1933 he published *The Mass Psychology of Fascism*, and was forced to flee to Norway when the Nazis came to power. There he pursued proof of the reality of orgasm energy, which he came to call orgone, but once again provoked controversy with experiments in which he hooked up to electrodes the genitals of kissing couples. Another scientist, Wilhelm Hoffman, tried to apply these techniques to schizophrenic patients, and in 1937 the Norwegian media conflated the two men's work, so that Reich found himself accused of experimenting on mental patients having sex.

In 1939 he fled once more, to America, where he set up home at an estate in Maine he named Organon. Here he developed his theories that all illness is caused by disruption in the flow of orgone, and invented technologies for capturing and concentrating the orgone energy he believed permeated the universe. Reich claimed that orgone 'accumulator boxes'

– wooden boxes lined with metal – could gather orgone energy, and that sitting inside one could treat and cure illness. Convinced by his own experiments (which appeared to show that temperatures inside a box were higher than those outside), Reich secured an interview with Albert Einstein to attempt to interest him in the new technology. The great physicist did some experiments of his own but soon concluded there was nothing to it, much to Reich's irritation. 'I sensed his weaknesses,' Reich recorded in his diary with characteristic modesty, 'and was aware when his opinions were incorrect but felt not a trace of gloating. I was proud of myself for that.'

Undaunted, Reich began manufacturing boxes, distributing them to doctors for a nominal fee. He also began to campaign noisily about the corrupt alliance between mainstream medicine, the pharmaceutical industry and the regulatory authorities that were supposed to prevent corruption – notably the FDA.

But he was on thin ice. Articles raking over the old coals of his Norwegian scandals surfaced periodically, linking him with rumours of crazed orgies and deviant sexual science, and now he was goading a federal agency at the height of anti-Communist paranoia in the US. The FDA launched an all-out assault on him, focusing on his claims that orgone accumulator boxes could treat illness. In 1954 Reich was banned from promoting his boxes, and his books were also banned. All the while his psyche was becoming more fragile; according to (sympathetic) biographer Robert Corrington he was suffering from hypomania, a form of mania characterized by wild enthusiasms, high sex drive and 'psychic inflation' (basically an out-of-control ego).

In 1956, after an associate had committed the extremely minor infraction of moving some orgone boxes across state lines, Reich disastrously mishandled the ensuing court case; he was drinking heavily and afflicted with a messiah complex. According to Corrington, 'He became persuaded that he was called to bear the burdens for a sexually starved and sadistic human race and that he could point the way to a new humanity if only his healing message could be heard'. Reich was convicted of contempt of court and sentenced to two years in jail. Federal agents trashed his laboratory, destroyed his stock of boxes and sent piles of his books to the incinerator.

In March 1957, Reich entered prison, and although he managed to write another book from his cell, he died a few months later of heart failure, probably exacerbated by the stress of confinement. At his funeral the eulogies painted him as a new messiah: 'Once in a thousand years, nay once in two thousand years, such a man comes upon this earth to change the destiny of the human race', intoned one of the speakers.

RORSCHACH TEST

The Rorschach ink-blot test is a projective test comprising ten abstract shapes made by dropping ink onto paper and folding it in half, so that they are bilaterally symmetrical. It is said to be a projective test because the person taking the test supposedly projects his or her personality and/or unconscious onto the ink blots: the pictures themselves are formless and meaningless, but the interpretation is loaded with meaning.

THE TEST WAS CREATED by Swiss psychiatrist Hermann Rorschach (1884–1922), a contemporary of Jung's who studied religious sects but also developed his eponymous test, perhaps inspired by his artistic background. As a teenager he was known for his painting, and by a curious coincidence his

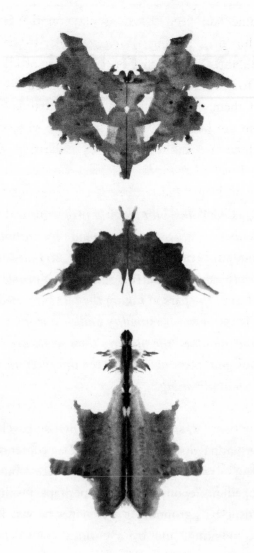

nickname had been 'Klex', a play on the German word for 'daubing' but also very similar to the word for 'inkblot'. Rorschach whittled his set of ink blots down to fifteen, although his publisher then discarded five of them, leaving the ten still used today. (Five of them are black and white, two have some colour and three are multi-coloured.) Publication of his book *Psychodiagnostik* (1921) was delayed by further problems and by the time it came out he was already dissatisfied with it, dying soon after of peritonitis.

Although his promising career was cut short, Rorschach's test has had a curious afterlife, exercising great fascination over lay people and psychiatrists alike. In popular conception it stands as a symbol of the mystic power of psychology, in which the shaman-like therapist can unlock the secrets of the psyche, using the ink blots like a diviner's bones or the entrails of a sacrifice. Amongst professionals it has generated a vast literature, spawning complex systems of interpretation. For instance, response to colour supposedly reflects emotional responsiveness, while seeing movement in the image reflects a tendency to introversion. Original but unusual interpretations signal neurotic tendencies. A subject who sees half-human, half-animal figures is supposedly in danger of developing schizophrenia.

In traditional application of the test, the therapist alone is the arbiter of the meaning and diagnostic value of the responses, but criticisms that this is subjective and lacks validity have led to development of supposedly standardized scoring systems. Critics point out that these have no validity either and are not backed up by any convincing studies (it is hard to see how they could be, given that the test, by definition, concerns subjective interpretations, and subjective interpretations of those interpretations), but this has not stopped claims that the Rorschach test can even be used to tell who is psychopathic and who is not.

Outside of a core of enthusiasts, the Rorschach and other projective tests are today regarded as pseudoscience on a par with graphology or crystal gazing, with which they share many characteristics. While such tests may help facilitate productive discussions between therapists and therapees, the ink blots themselves have no special value; therapists might as well ask their clients to look at clouds or stains on the carpet.

SKINNER BOX

An experimental apparatus designed by the US psychologist B. F. Skinner (1904–1990) in 1929.

IN ITS BASIC FORM it is a cube around 30 cm on each side, light and sound-proofed to isolate the animal inside (usually a rat) from disturbances and ensure that the experimenter controls the stimuli presented to the test subject. Inside the box is a device called an operandum or manipulandum, a lever, button or bar that the animal can operate, and a device to deliver rewards, such as a food hopper or water tube. Using this apparatus an animal can be trained or conditioned to work the operandum in return for rewards, known as positive reinforcement. This kind of training or learning is called operant conditioning. Adaptions to the Skinner box include electrified floors, to produce

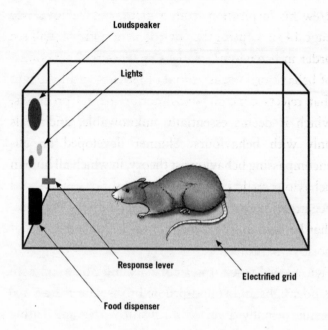

Loudspeaker

Lights

Response lever

Electrified grid

Food dispenser

negative reinforcement, and speakers/screens to present stimuli such as natural scenes or music.

A similar device known as the Thorndike puzzle box, invented by E.L. Thorndike, is generally considered to be less 'pure' in design and effect. The point of the Skinner box is to experiment with an animal, yet still achieve the level of experimental control seen in more rigorous sciences such as physics or chemistry. Skinner drew his inspiration from a dictum of Pavlov's (see page 143): 'control the environment and you will see order in behaviour'. He was a committed proponent of behaviourism, the school of psychological thought that rejects concern with interior mental processes, which it deems essentially unknowable, and deals only with behaviours. Skinner developed an all-encompassing behaviourist theory, in which all human behaviour could be explained in terms of positive and negative reinforcement. He explained, for instance, that he held to his particular lecture style because of positive reinforcement (i.e. the audience liked it). In fact, according to operant-conditioning theory there is no such thing as free will, and our mental lives are merely window dressing to behaviours controlled by feedback loops.

Theory was something of a dirty word for Skinner; he was more interested in applications. During World War Two he devised Project Pigeon (aka Project Orcon, for 'organic control'), known as the 'pigeons in a pelican' programme. Operant-conditioning methods were used to train pigeons to guide missiles by pecking at the centre of an image of the target. Amazingly it worked but was never pursued by the military. Skinner also applied his theories to his own children, famously building a 'baby box' or 'air crib' for his infant daughter as a kind of germ-free play pen in which operant-conditioning techniques could be used to entertain and educate her. Inevitably his baby box became conflated in the public mind with the Skinner box for rats; Skinner objected to both this development and the name given to his experimental apparatus.

SLEEP PARALYSIS

The phenomenon in which someone waking from or falling to sleep, but not actually asleep, finds themselves unable to move.

BECAUSE THIS PARALYSIS OCCURS during hypna-gogic and hypnopompic states (the transitional states of consciousness experienced on falling to and waking from sleep), it can be accompanied by auditory and visual hallucinations, hallucinations of presence (i.e. the feeling that someone or something is present though unseen), intense fear and anxiety, floating and discorporeal sensations and feelings of suffocation and/or the sensation of a crushing pressure on the chest.

If this list of associated symptoms sounds similar to descriptions of paranormal and supernatural experiences such as alien abduction, night hag visitations and incubus/succubus demonic visitations, this is probably not a coincidence. Consider a typical alien abduction experience. The victim is in bed and finds himself awake but unable to move; he senses an alien presence, just beyond the periphery of his vision, which is observing him with malign intent; he hears strange buzzing and rushing noises, sees a bright light and is gripped around the chest; he begins to float and somehow passes through the wall to experience a vivid flying-saucer visit, then finds himself back in bed, shaken but with no physical evidence of the abduction. This sequence precisely describes a sleep-paralysis event, filtered through the lens of cultural familiarity with the tropes of science fiction and UFO lore. In earlier times, a similar sequence of sensations accompanied visits from spectral terrors such as the night hag, a hideous entity that sits on the sleeper's chest, crushing and choking them (as famously depicted in the painting *The Nightmare* by Henry Fuseli); or the succubus and her male counterpart, the incubus, demons who came in the night to straddle their victims and steal their precious bodily fluids.

Sleep paralysis is surprisingly common, occurring in at least forty to fifty per cent of normal individuals sometime during their lifetimes, and afflicting a small minority on a regular basis. It is much more common in narcoleptics, where it is associated with daytime paralysis known as cataplexy; seventeen to forty of narcoleptics experience frequent episodes of sleep paralysis.

SPINAL BLOCK

Sleep paralysis is believed to be due to persistence of REM atonia into the hypnagogic/ hypnopompic state. Atonia is a clinical term for paralysis of the skeletal muscles, which kicks in during REM sleep so that dreams are not acted out. Parts of the lower brain called the subcoerulear and magnocellular nuclei block the spinal nerves from activating skeletal muscles, so that REM sleepers can only breathe, move their eyes and twitch their extremities. The opposite of sleep paralysis could be said to be REM behaviour disorder, which is where the mechanism of REM atonia fails and people are able to act out their dreams, leading to sleepwalking and other potentially dangerous behaviours.

SPLIT-BRAIN STUDIES

A split brain is one in which the corpus callosum has been severed. The corpus callosum is a thick band of over 600 million nerve fibres that acts as a bridge between the two hemispheres of the brain.

THE HUMAN BRAIN is distinguished by its massive cerebrum, the wrinkled, walnut-like outer layer of the brain, where all of the higher functions from vision, hearing and touch to language, planning and problem-solving reside. The cerebrum is divided into two halves, the left and right hemispheres, and it has been known since the advent of brain-damage studies that the hemispheres seem to have different functions and domains of control. Normally they are joined by bridges of connecting nerves called commissures, so that nerve traffic can pass quickly from one side to the other, but in a split-brain patient the largest of these commissures, the corpus callosum, has been severed in an operation known as a commissurotomy. As a result the two hemispheres cannot communicate with each other as normal, and clever experiments have revealed profound effects on perception, thinking and consciousness.

Left Hemisphere

Right Hemisphere

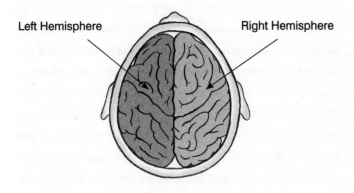

Commissurotomies have been carried out on a small number of patients with very severe epilepsy, where it was hoped that cutting the corpus callosum would help to limit the spread of the electrical 'brain storms' that afflicted them. Initially psychologists hoping for revelations about the nature of consciousness and cognitive organisation were disappointed when the first studies of split-brain patients appeared to show that they were unchanged, but this was probably because the perceptions of the patients were not controlled. If split-brain patients can move their heads about and use both hands in tasks, both sides of the brain can acquire the same perceptions and any separation in activities can easily be circumvented.

In the 1950s, Roger Sperry began experimenting with split-brain cats, in which the optic nerves had been surgically divided so that each eye only communicated with one hemisphere. He showed that when such a cat learned to perform a task with one hemisphere, the other hemisphere possessed no knowledge of it. It was even possible to get a cat to make opposite choices with each hemisphere. In the 1960s Sperry and colleagues were invited to test commissurotomy patients (Sperry would later receive a Nobel prize for his research), and devised elegant experiments in which information was available to only one hemisphere at a time. For instance, your left hand is controlled by the right hemisphere of your brain, and your right visual field (i.e. things seen on the right of the visual field of each eye) is seen by your left brain. The split-brain patients were presented with tasks such as naming objects held in their left hands, or rhyming with words presented to their right visual field.

The experiments showed that there were profound differences between the hemispheres. The right-brain has little access to language, and is unable to produce speech, so that, for instance, an object held in the left hand could not be described. The left-brain struggles to recognize faces unless they have clear distinguishing features such as a moustache or glasses. The right-brain can understand single words but not complex sentences, and cannot rhyme. The patients themselves did not seem to be aware of these deficits, and would typically come up with explanations, for example, they would claim their left hand had 'lost its sensitivity' when unable to name what it was holding.

In particular, the left-brain hosts a device called the 'interpreter', which always tries to piece together a coherent story and confabulates explanations of choices made by the right-brain, of which it seems to lack conscious awareness. In one test the non-verbal right-brain was shown a picture of a snow scene and presented with cards to choose, the patient picking a shovel card with his left hand. The left brain was shown a chicken's foot and chose a chicken. When asked to explain the choices, the patient explained, 'the chicken claw goes with the chicken, and you need a shovel to clean out the chicken shed'. The left-brain didn't know what the right-brain had seen or why it had picked the shovel, but came up with a story.

The left-brain proves to be dominant for language, problem solving, logic, mathematics and explanations, narratives, reasoning, etc. It is said to be more analytic. The right-brain is more synthetic; it perceives things as a whole or gestalt, including faces and complex shapes, and is more literal in interpreting and therefore remembering events.

TWO FOR THE PRICE OF ONE

Interestingly, split-brain patients are better at some tasks than people with intact commissures. Having two independent perceptual systems acting at once means that it takes a split-brain patient half the time to scan a given number of pictures when they are presented to each hemisphere separately as it does when they are all presented to one side, and split-brain patients can outperform normal individuals in a test of visual retention when the information is distributed between the two visual half-fields (i.e. each hemisphere gets its own information feed).

Despite these differences split-brain patients do not experience divided consciousness. It has been suggested that they have less access to their own emotions, presumably because much emotional response is generated in the right hemisphere but cannot be described or interpreted in words by the left brain. On the other hand emotional states are able to pass between the hemispheres through the lower parts of the brain, such as the brainstem, which remain connected, and through the physiology and actions of the body. Similarly both hemispheres experience the same external world, and this helps to unify them.

The findings of split-brain studies certainly seem to provide the basis for the popular stereotypes about left-brain, right-brain oppositions (e.g. rational versus emotional, maths versus art). But split-brain researchers dismiss these as oversimplifications. Deeper questions about the nature and seat of consciousness remain unanswered, but split-brain patients certainly give no evidence of having 'two people inside one head'.

STANFORD PRISON EXPERIMENT

Also known as the Zimbardo prison experiment because the lead researcher was Philip Zimbardo (b. 1933), this is one of the most famous experiments in psychology.

ZIMBARDO WAS INTERESTED in the psychology of aggressive behaviour and social accountability for behaviour. In a series of variations on the Milgram authority experiments (see page 138), he showed that people were more likely to give worse electric shocks to subjects if they wore lab coats and hoods versus people wearing their normal clothes and large name tags.

From this he moved on to an experiment that would look at how people behaved in prisons. There were many stories of prison guards abusing prisoners

– was this bad behaviour down to the pathology of people who choose to be guards or because prisoners somehow brought it on themselves? The resulting experiment would suggest that in fact it was a third variable, the institution itself, which elicited aggressive behaviour.

In 1971 Zimbardo advertised for healthy young men to take part in a prison experiment for $15 per day. Extensive testing suggested they were all psychologically healthy, and they were randomly assigned to be either prisoners or guards. Once they had agreed to participate, the prisoners were 'arrested' at their homes and treated like real criminals: fingerprinted and booked, stripped and deloused, and made to wear prison gowns, tight-fitting nylon caps and chains around their ankles. They were confined in the basement of the Stanford University psychology department, which had been fitted out to resemble a real prison with barred doors and windows, bare cells and an 'isolation unit'. Before any of this began, however, the participants were informed of their right to call a halt to the experiment and leave at any time. Meanwhile prisoners and guards alike had been informed that roles had been randomly assigned, so they knew that the prisoners had done nothing wrong.

The guards were given beige uniforms, truncheons and mirrored glasses. They were told not to use physical violence but apart from this were simply directed to keep the prisoners incarcerated. Within hours, however, the guards began to act out their roles in aggressive fashion, abusing prisoners and forcibly breaking up a 'rebellion' in which prisoners refused to leave their cells. Very quickly the two groups settled into stereotypical roles, with the guards becoming aggressive, cruel and sadistic, and the prisoners passive, withdrawn and submissive. The prisoners seemed to forget that they had the right to leave, obsessing over prison rules and regulations that the guards themselves had drawn up, and meekly accepting the rejection of their 'petition for parole'. One prisoner went on hunger strike and was confined to solitary. Guards began to conspire to humiliate target prisoners (by stripping them, putting bags over their heads and making them do press-ups), and at least a third of them displayed genuinely sadistic tendencies. Some prisoners became so emotionally traumatized that they had to be removed and although the experiment was supposed to run for two weeks, Zimbardo shut it down after six days.

The Stanford prison experiment was and has remained deeply controversial, with criticism over ethical considerations and a supposed lack of informed consent from the participants. In Zimbardo's defence it is suggested that there was no way he could have ensured such consent, given that he did not know what was about to happen. The experiment provided compelling evidence that individual personality variables are not the cause of behaviours associated with institutions – Zimbardo had controlled for these variables by randomly assigning the recruits to the experimental groups. Instead the nature of the institution itself appears to influence behaviour by setting and scripting 'roles' for the various 'actors' within. People in institutions such as prisons seem to follow a sort of 'psychologic', very possibly at odds with any presumption of institutional rationality. Yet at the same time, the experiment seems to offer chilling evidence that anyone can be transformed into a sadist simply by putting on a pair of mirrored shades and a uniform.

It may be that the experiment itself is not robust enough to bear the weight of these conclusions. It had a relatively tiny sample size, was not completed and cannot be properly replicated. A study based on the Stanford prison experiment was performed in 2001–2 and filmed by the BBC, but there were significant differences and the findings were not comparable.

STOCKHOLM SYNDROME

The condition where victims of kidnapping, hostage-taking or other related situations come to identify and sympathize with their captors.

THE NAME COMES from the Sveriges Kreditbanken siege of 1973, in which two men held up a bank in Stockholm and kept four bank employees hostage for five and a half days in a 3m by 14m vault. The captors and the hostages were confined in close quarters for 131 hours. The authorities were amazed to find the hostages apparently resenting their efforts to resolve the siege, and defending the actions of the robbers. One of the hostages broke off her engagement and maintained a relationship with one of her former captors while he was in jail, and all four refused to testify against the robbers and even raised money for their defence.

Intrigued psychologists characterized this reaction as a form of defence mechanism, in which the hostage relieves the terror of imminent death and the profound stress of powerlessness by projecting positive feelings onto the captors and identifying with the aggressor, to use Freudian terminology. In psychoanalysis, identification with the aggressor is a defence mechanism in which intolerable anxiety caused by an external hostile force is relieved by internalising the force, so that for boys in the throes of the Oedipal complex the threatening father figure is internalized as the superego and the boy comes to identify with the values of his father. In Stockholm syndrome, siding with the captor may be a way for hostages to feel they have regained some control and at the same time relieves the tension caused by impotent rage and powerless enmity.

Research by the FBI indicates that the Stockholm syndrome has been overly hyped because it offers such a media and folk-psychology friendly narrative, and is in fact extremely rare with ninety-two per cent of hostage victims surveyed displaying no signs of the syndrome. The FBI also suggests a number of preconditions for development of Stockholm syndrome. The hostages must fear execution and then feel assured that they owe their survival to their captors, leading to feelings of gratitude. Hostages and captors must spend prolonged time in close contact, isolated from others. Most importantly, the captors must treat the hostages with kindness and not physically or psychologically abuse them.

This last condition is problematic for the most famous instance of apparent Stockholm syndrome. In 1974 a left-wing urban guerrilla group called the Symbionese Liberation Army kidnapped nineteen-year-old newspaper heiress Patty Hearst. Some months later, having adopted the pseudonym 'Tanya', she took part in a bank heist as part of the group, having apparently joined their crusade. Later she claimed to have been sexually abused and tortured by the SLA, and was widely held to have been brainwashed in a classic case of Stockholm syndrome. The term is also sometimes applied to victims of domestic abuse, who display similar behaviours, such as refusing to cooperate with law enforcement, making bail for perpetrators and otherwise remaining loyal to them.

SYNAESTHESIA

From the Greek for 'joining of the senses',
synaesthesia is the stimulation of one sense by
something experienced in another sense.

IN THE MOST COMMON TYPE of synaesthesia, numbers are also experienced as colours (e.g. five might be red, and two might be green). Another common type is hearing-colour synaesthesia, in which sounds, especially musical tones, are experienced as colours. Rare forms include tasting shapes and feeling the texture of tastes. Synaesthesia is one way (i.e. for a number-colour synaesthete, colours do not trigger numbers), and its hallmark is that the sensory correspondences are stable. In other words, a synaesthete would say that the five is 'red' every time, even when retested after many years.

Scientific interest in the phenomenon dates to the late nineteenth century, most notably in the research of Francis Galton who wrote about synaesthesia in his *Inquiries into Human Faculty and Its Development* (1883). Galton deduced that the condition is inherited since it seemed to run in families, and it is now believed to have a genetic basis. Estimates of its prevalence have mainly been in the range one in 10,000 to one in 1,000, but a more recent study suggests that it could be as common as one in 200. People who have synaesthesia from birth are said to be developmentally synaesthetic, but it can also be acquired through brain damage and drug use. Women report having synaesthesia six times more frequently than men, but this may not reflect the actual sex ratio, which is probably much more even.

Literary evidence of synaesthesia extends back to the earliest written works. In the works of Homer, for instance, the voices of cicadas are described as 'lily-like' and Odysseus's words fall like 'winter snowflakes'. Perhaps the best-known synaesthetic work is Arthur Rimbaud's sonnet *Voyelles* ('Vowels') beginning 'A noir, E blanc, I rouge, U vert, O bleu . . .' But are these literary manifestations merely instances of metaphor? In fact, is synaesthesia a genuine sensory phenomenon or just a confabulation involving persistent metaphors or learned associations?

Evidence that it *is* a genuine sensory phenomenon comes from a task where a triangle of twos is presented against a background field of fives. Non-synaesthetes find it very hard to spot the twos because they are mirror images of fives, let alone spotting the shape spelled out by the twos; number-colour synaesthetes on the other hand, spot the shapes easily, as, say a green triangle against a red background, and complete the task dramatically more quickly than normal subjects.

Testing has also revealed fascinating distinctions between types of synaesthesia. For some number-colour synaesthetes, for instance, colour is only evoked when viewing an Arabic-Hindu numeral, and not a Roman numeral, whereas others get colour evoked by a number in whatever form it comes – sometimes even with ordered things such as days of the week. Clearly the synaesthesia is operating at different levels of mental processing in these two types.

Brain imaging shows that the common synaesthesia pairings (e.g. numbers and colours) are processed by neighbouring brain regions, suggesting that synaesthetes have inherited a gene that somehow creates connections between regions that are not normally linked. (This in turn suggests that foot fetishism may be a form of synaesthesia, because the brain regions containing the touch receptors for the feet and the genitals are next to each other.) The most likely scenario is that the gene disrupts the pruning process that moulds the brain in early brain development, including neural separation of the senses. This 'neuronal pruning' theory is supported by evidence that very young babies may have synaesthesia. For instance, babies given bumpy or smooth dummies to suck on preferred to look at a picture of the same-texture dummy – somehow they could infer the appearance of the dummy from its texture.

Is synaesthesia more than just a curiosity? Its increased prevalence amongst artistic and creative people suggests the gene for it may survive because it confers some sort of evolutionary advantage. It may be that synaesthesia is simply an extreme form of an ability possessed by all humans, which underlies the ability to make connections between abstract concepts and make abstract connections between concepts, so that the investigation and elucidation of synaesthesia can tell us much about the evolution of metaphor and abstract thinking. It could even shed light on the fundamental mystery of consciousness – as pointed out by one of the leading researchers into synaesthesia, psychologist Simon Baron-Cohen: 'synaesthesia may teach us how unusual wiring in the brain can lead to altered perception, and how genes may affect subjective experience'.

THEORY OF MIND

Also known as mind-reading and folk psychology, theory of mind (ToM) is how people understand their own and others' mental states, including thoughts, beliefs, desires and emotions.

ANY TIME THAT YOU THINK about why you or someone else did something, you employ ToM, a set of tools, possibly rules, which allow you to imagine what is going on inside people's heads. ToM is an aspect of mental functioning usually taken for granted, perhaps because almost everyone does it all the time (hence its description as 'folk psychology'), but it raises fascinating questions about the nature of consciousness, its evolution and who does and doesn't have ToM.

The first to discuss ToM were the primatologists David Premack and Guy Woodruff, in a 1978 paper 'Does the chimpanzee have a theory of mind?' They wanted to know if chimps thought like we did – they seem to be quite good at understanding other people's behaviour, but could they impute states of mind? The evidence seems to be that they can't: for instance, when they have to decide who to ask for food out of someone who can see where the food is kept and someone whose eyes are covered, they seem to guess at random.

So it seems that chimps do not have a ToM, but at what stage do humans develop one? Premack and Woodruff's paper triggered intense research interest, particularly around the ability to attribute false beliefs. This is where you are able to understand that someone else might believe something you know to be false, i.e. they can hold a false belief. In the classic Sally–Anne experiment, children are shown two dolls. Sally hides a ball in a covered basket, watched by Anne. When Sally goes out for a walk, Anne moves the ball to a box. Then Sally comes back and the children are asked, 'Where will Sally look for the ball?' Children under three think she will look in the box, whereas children aged four and over are able

This is Sally   This is Anne

Sally puts the ball in her basket

Sally goes away

Anne moves the ball to her box

Where will Sally look for her ball?

to attribute a false belief to Sally, and recognize that she will look for the ball where she falsely believes it to be – in the basket. An important finding is that autistic children, including older ones, typically fail the Sally–Anne test, suggesting that their condition involves and may even be caused by 'mind blindness' or failure to develop ToM.

There are two main explanations of how ToM works. One school of thought – known somewhat confusingly as the 'theory theory of mind' – is that children literally develop theories about how others think, like little scientists. As they learn more about cognition and emotion their theories become more sophisticated. Another explanation is that ToM works through simulation or modelling – we simulate what other people might be thinking based on our knowledge of our own minds.

ToM has clear implications for the evolution of intelligence and consciousness. Individuals who are able to predict and manipulate others' states of mind are at a great advantage. On the one hand they can lie, while on the other hand they can successfully influence others' emotions and be influenced by them (known as empathy by emotional contagion), which in turn motivates positive or 'prosocial' actions. So

ToM might be at the root of both the Machiavellian intelligence hypothesis (that social intelligence becomes increasingly evolutionarily advantageous as social networks become increasingly complex) and of the cooperative principle governing human interactions.

Scientists searching for the neural basis of ToM have found some specific areas of the brain light up during tasks such as false belief attribution: specifically the temporoparietal junction (TPJ) and the medial parietal and prefrontal cortex. Also involved may be mirror neurons: nerve cells that fire both when you perform an action or experience a cognition *and* when you observe someone else doing the same. Dysfunctional mirror neurons are implicated in autism, and it may be that they are crucial to the operation of ToM.

TURING TEST

A test of whether a computer can carry on a conversation well enough for a human interlocutor to be unable to distinguish it from another human.

NAMED AFTER THE MATHEMATICIAN and father of computing, Alan Turing (1912–1954), who proposed a thought experiment he called the 'imitation game' in an article in 1950.

Turing was addressing the question, 'can a machine be intelligent?', but dismissed it as 'too meaningless to deserve discussion'. After all, what is meant by 'intelligence'? Instead Turing proposed that if a machine could *appear* to be as intelligent as a human, then for all intents and purposes it could be considered as intelligent as a human. He referred to an imitation game in which a man tries to answer questions as he thinks a woman would, and a questioner tries to tell the imitator apart from a real woman by means of written questions and answers. Substituting a computer for the imitating man, Turing suggested that if an interlocutor is allowed to ask wide-ranging and penetrating questions via text, and cannot on the basis of the answers given distinguish a computer respondent from a human one, then the computer could be said to be, in some senses, intelligent.

Turing thought that by 2000 machine intelligence would be able to pass this test seventy per cent of the time. In practice no machine has ever come close, highlighting the difficulty of the task facing those attempting to engineer artificial intelligence (AI). The Turing test has been more fruitful in stimulating debate about the nature of intelligence, and what it means to talk about artificial or machine intelligence.

The Turing test suggests a behaviourist-style approach to intelligence, with an intelligence seen as a sort of 'black box' into which you feed questions and out of which come answers. This sort of input/output or I/O model says that what's inside the black box isn't important, only the inputs and outputs matter. It's an approach that has been criticized for missing essential qualities of intelligence, most notably by the philosopher John Searle in his Chinese Room thought experiment. Searle imagined a man in a room who speaks no Chinese, but is passed Chinese messages through a slot in the wall. Using a big book of syntactical rules written in English he is able to process the Chinese symbols into answers, which he posts back out of the slot. To a Chinese interlocutor outside the room he seems to speak Chinese, but in fact he has no semantic understanding of Chinese. Similarly, Searle argues, a machine intelligence passing the Turing test is processing language to produce answers, but has no real semantic understanding.

The cognitive scientist Robert French points out that the Turing test need not be a simple pass or fail, all or nothing affair. What if a computer was good enough to fool a human questioner for an hour before being rumbled? We might classify such a machine as more intelligent than one that failed the test after a minute. French also points out that the test may be unfair on computers, since human intelligence, particularly in terms of its expression in language and conversation, could be inextricably linked to biological and concrete qualities such as embodiment and physical interaction with the world. He suggests that a machine intelligence would have no context to deal with questions such as 'Is a mouthful of cold soda more like having pins and needles in your feet or cold water on your head?'

Hugh Loebner has offered a cash prize to a team who can program a computer to pass the Turing test, but in annual competitions none come close. In fact the field has not progressed much since the celebrated ELIZA, a program written by Joseph Weizenbaum around 1965. In one of its modes, called DOCTOR, it imitated a Rogerian psychotherapist by using its simple programming to turn statements into questions. For instance, if the user typed in 'I feel sad', DOCTOR might respond, 'Why do you feel sad?' ELIZA was remarkably good at fooling people, some of whom would continue to interact with the program as if it were sentient, even after its nature

> Hello, I am Eliza. What do you want to talk about?

was explained. There is even evidence that people using a program similar to DOCTOR can get as much benefit as from a real psychotherapist, which can be seen as part satire on/part critique of/part insight into the nature and worth of talking therapies.

BIBLIOGRAPHY

Bayne, Tim (ed); *Oxford Companion to Consciousness* (OUP, 2009)

Blakemore, Colin (ed); *Oxford Companion to the Body* (OUP, 2002)

Colman, Andrew M.; *Dictionary of Psychology* (OUP, 2009)

Craighead, W. Edward (ed); *Concise Corsini Encyclopaedia of Psychology and Behavioral Science* (Wiley, 2004)

Davey, Graham; *Encyclopaedic Dictionary of Psychology* (Hodder Education, 2006)

Gregory, Richard L; *Oxford Companion to the Mind* (OUP, 2004)

Hamblin, Jacob Darwin; *Science in the Early Twentieth Century: An Encyclopaedia* (ABC-CLIO, 2005)

Harre, Rom; *Key Thinkers in Psychology* (Sage, 2005)

Hopkins, Brian (ed); *Cambridge Encyclopaedia of Child Development* (Cambridge, 2005)

Kurtz, Lester (ed); *Encyclopaedia of Violence, Peace and Conflict* (Elsevier, 2008)

Levy, Joel; *Scientific Feuds* (New Holland, 2010)

Levy, Joel; *Why? Answers to Everyday Scientific Questions* (Michael O'Mara, 2012)

McLeish, Kenneth (ed); *Bloomsbury Guide to Human Thought* (Bloomsbury, 1993)

Nadel, L; *Encyclopaedia of Cognitive Science* (Wiley, 2002)

Reber, Arthur S; *Penguin Dictionary of Psychology* (Penguin, 2009)

Reynolds, Cecil R. (ed); *Encyclopaedia of Special Education: A Reference for the Education of Children, Adolescents, and Adults with Disabilities and Other Exceptional Individuals* (Wiley, 2007)

Roeckelein, J.E. (ed); *Elsevier's Dictionary of Psychological Theories* (Elsevier, 2006)

Rosario, V.A. and Pillard, Richard; *Homosexuality and Science: A Guide to the Debates* (ABC-CLIO, 2002)

Skelton, Ross (ed); *Edinburgh International Encyclopaedia of Psychoanalysis* (Edinburgh University Press, 2010)

Websites

Simply Psychology; www.simplypsychology.org
Skeptic's Dictionary; www.skepdic.com
Medical Anthropology: http://anthro.palomar.edu/
 medical/default.htm
International Society for the Study of Trauma and
 Dissociation: www.isst-d.org
The Psychologist: www.thepsychologist.org.uk

INDEX